IT SURE 'NUFF HAPPENED:

I Was There

Alan Easley

NukeWorks
Publishing

NukeWorks Publishing
Fulton, Mo 65251 USA

ISBN 978-0-9825294-8-5

Cover design by Justin Easley
Cover photos by Justin Easley

Some stories have been previously published in various magazines, etc. These stories are used with permission of the original publishers.

All photos used with permission of their respective owners.

Printed in U.S.A.

IN MEMORY

This book is dedicated to the memory of my longtime friend, neighbor, and tractor pulling buddy, Bill Blackwell, who died September 7, 2016. Bill kept asking me when this book was going to be done; I wish to hell he was still here to read it!

ACKNOWLEDGEMENTS

Once again thanks to my Grandson, Justin, for scanning all of the pictures contained in this book, for taking the cover photo and designing the cover, and getting all of this stuff set up in book form. I don't quite understand how it works, but he gets it done.

Thanks to my Granddaughter-in-law, Amanda, for all of her typing expertise. Somehow, between working full time and being pregnant, she found time to do this for me. If you'd seen some of the handwritten stories that I handed her you'd wonder how she ever figured them out.

Also, thanks to all of the people who sort of pushed me into writing a second book: James Earl and David Grant; "Easley, why didn't you mention ____?" Well, I didn't think about it, that's why. And Charlie Lee; "Alan, do you remember when we were working on the Moberly Prison and ____?" Yeah Charlie, I remember that. And Joe Baumgartner; "Alan, do you remember when J.R. bought that Shorthorn bull and ____?" I'd forgot all about that Joe, but I remember it now. And the list goes on. I just needed a few people to jog my memory, such as it is. They did a pretty good job of it, and this is the result. If you don't like my book blame them, they made me do it.

Also, thanks to the magazine editors who graciously gave me permission to use some previously published stories in the book. And to Joe G. Dillard, author of "A Full Cup of Joe," for coining the phrase "FA WHOOSH" and allowing me to use it.

And last but not least, to my childhood neighbor and lifelong friend, John Cavcey, for his illustrations that are used in this book. When I didn't have the right picture to go with a story, he quickly produced one. When you get right down to it, all I did was remember some stuff, everyone else did all the hard work and I sure 'nuff appreciate it!

INTRODUCTION

When you're born on a farm that has been in the family since the 1840's, and then spend 70 some years in the same area there are lots of things to remember, but by the time I finished my first book I thought I'd pretty much remembered them all. However, it seems like I'd only scratched the surface. People would ask me "why didn't you mention this?" or "why didn't you mention that?" I'd tell them because I didn't think about it, and then I'd make a little note for future reference. Apparently I made it to the future, so I'm mentioning it now.

If you don't like me writing about something you did, maybe you shouldn't have done it in the first place, because from dogs to kids to neighbors, nothing or nobody, including myself, gets any special treatment, because "IT SURE 'NUFF HAPPENED: I was there."

FOREWORD

Alan Easley has accomplished what many of us wish we could do in writing this book. He can tell a story with history, humor and ease in an entertaining style. The combination of those ingredients, plus the brevity of each story, will send the reader through a gamut of emotions – laughing so hard you cry, cringing to the point of wanting to disappear (Alan has never opened a can of varnish), and yearning for a simpler, steadier time – all in the brief span of a few minutes.

It's fun to know the "characters" in life because they add needed flavor to a stressed-out world. Alan is one of those characters. He didn't train for it; he was born to it. It's not the most important part of him; it's just the part he can't help. The most important part of Alan is that he's the kind of Boone County boy and Missouri man who cares deeply about his family, his community and his country. His obvious love of life and the people in it is found on almost every page.

If you're "country-raised," you'll see a lot of your favorite past in these stories. And if you're not, you'll get a glimpse of what you missed.

Roger B. Wilson
52nd Governor of the State of Missouri

IT SURE 'NUFF HAPPENED:

I Was There

The Olivet Neighborhood

In my book, "It Must Be True: Paw-Paw Said So," I told about how the old neighborhood on Bearfield Road has changed since I was a kid. The Olivet neighborhood has changed every bit as much since Marcia and I moved here in 1963.

Jim Myers sold his place south of WW to Emory Sapp, and it's now covered by El Chaparral Subdivision, Casey's Store, a small shopping center, a church and Cedar Ridge School. East of Jim's was the old Estes Place that I farmed for several years. It's now pretty much covered with houses, and it's also home to the new Elks Club building.

Ray and Eva Hinshaw raised horned Herefords on their farm until they were up in their 90's. It's now the "Vineyards" subdivision. As far as I know, there's not a grapevine within five miles, but it's still the "Vineyards". Eutsy Johnson's coal mine farm is now the home of Old Hawthorne Golf Course, and a bunch of really big assed houses. The Murphy farm that I rented for 20 some years has been split into 10 and 20 acre tracts, and the 40 acre Olivet Church farm is now 4 tracts.

Everything that Charles Henry Reid owned east of Rangeline Road has been chopped all to hell, and likewise the place R.J. Estes had on the southeast corner of Rangeline and Turner Farm Road. NASCAR driver Carl

Edwards now owns the old Schwabe Farm at the east end of Turner Farm Road, that Bill Schuler and I farmed for over 20 years. He has built an airstrip, hangar, and has a 15-foot-high privacy fence across the front of the property. There is some pretty thin ground on that old place, it'll probably make a better landing strip than it did a crop farm.

Hugh Tincher bought 50-some acres off the south end of Henry Forsee's place, and sold it off in 10-acre lots. It has some really nice homes on it. James Earl Grant and I rented that piece of ground from Hugh for several years, before he started selling lots. We raised some pretty good milo on it one year.

J.R. Jacobs' place south of WW is also split into 10-acre lots. There are some nice houses there, but I think it looked better when it was covered with Shorthorn cattle.

Marcia and I have also done our part to chop up the neighborhood. Years ago, we sold 3 acres off the northwest corner of our place to Tom and Velda Davison, and they were great neighbors for 20 years before they sold it and moved to town. During the dirty 80's we sold 80 acres off the east side of our farm to Gary and Jan Hayes. About 5 years before Marcia died, we sold 10 acres off the west side to Greg and Jamie, so some of our grandkids lived real close for a few years. Those four are now married or in the service, Army, Navy and Marines.

Don Wemhoff still has the place across the road that he bought from Arno Winkler, but one of these days Boone County or the City of Columbia will build a sewer line pretty close, and I 'spect that will be the end of another farm.

I won't see it happen, but the time will come when a person will drive from Kansas City to St. Louis without ever seeing a farm. It'll just be one big assed development from one side of the state to the other. Damn, ain't progress wonderful?

Way Back When

NOTE: Some of the stories in **Way Back When** *overlap with stories in* **Back When**. *I just wasn't real sure where some of them went. I guess it doesn't really matter, either way it's been quite a spell since it happened.*

Back in the 1920's and '30's there was a strip mine on the north end of the farm that Eutsy Johnson sold to Billy Sapp, where Old Hawthorne Golf Course is located now.

The mine was north of the creek, and Bryan Mitchel told me that the hill on the south side of the creek was so steep that one team couldn't pull a wagon load of coal up the hill. Bryan said that the mine kept a good team and a driver at the foot of the hill whenever the mine was open, and the team spent all day, every day, helping pull loaded wagons up the hill, then being led back to the creek to wait for the next load.

I've hauled several loads of wheat up that hill, and the old GMC truck that I had at the time could have used a good team in front of it more than once.

*   *   *   *   *

Bryan also told me there was a vein of coal in the south bank of the little creek that runs through Ray and Eva Hinshaw's farm (now "The Vineyards" subdivision). In the 1930's during the depression no one had any money to buy coal, so the neighbors all dug their coal from the vein by the creek. Bryan said it was pretty low quality, and left a lot of clinkers when it burned, but it was free and it sure beat no coal at all.

Bryan said the vein was dug out for several hundred yards along the creek bank, and then it suddenly turned straight down. After following it down for about 15 feet they tapped a vein of water and the pit filled up. That was the end of the free coal, but it was good while it lasted.

*   *   *   *   *

Fred Barnes never talked much about his time in the service, but he did tell me about a wild motorcycle ride he took one afternoon.

Fred said his squad had been moved a couple of miles behind the lines for a few days of rest and recuperation. There was a captured German motorcycle in camp, and one day Fred got permission from his Sergeant to take it for a ride. He'd never ridden a motorcycle before, but he was puttering along, just enjoying doing something different for a change.

Fred told me that all of the roads in the area were raised 5' or 6' above the adjoining ground. He had gotten quite a ways from camp and as he rode along he suddenly heard the sound of an incoming artillery shell. Fred said it hit 40 yards or so shy of the road. He heard another one, and it overshot the road about the same distance. He suddenly realized they were shooting at him, and were about to get the range. He turned around and headed back to camp at full throttle, bent over the handlebars and holding on for all he was worth. Fred said the speedometer went up to 90 kilometers per hour, and it was pegged as he headed towards camp.

Everyone heard him coming, and they scattered as he blew between the tents at full throttle. He said it took him another 1/4 mile to get stopped, then he turned around and puttered back to camp. Fred said that was the first and last time he ever went for a ride on a captured motorcycle.

*   *   *   *   *

Fred also told me that at one time they went several weeks without having a hot meal. Their rations consisted of cans of soft cheese, with no crackers, and cans of beef stew.

He said that he got where he couldn't even stand to look at that cold greasy stew, much less eat it, so he was surviving on nothing but cheese. I won't go into the details, but when Fred told the story you laughed so hard that your ribs hurt. He said it took about a week in the camp medical facilities to get everything "worked out."

*   *   *   *   *

Pappy and Uncle Edward were fishing at Uncle Paul's one afternoon (on the farm that is now owned by Steve and Carolyn Cheavens) when they decided to flop down at a riffle and get a drink. Us kids were always told "never drink out of a creek, the water's dirty," but I guess it was OK for adults.

Pappy flopped down about 10 feet upstream from Uncle Edward, and after they got up Uncle Edward remarked that the water sure was sour tasting. They took a closer look at the creek and about two feet upstream from where Uncle Edward had drunk was a pile of fresh cow manure about an inch under the surface with the water flowing across it down to where Uncle Edward had drunk.

I 'spect that water did taste pretty sour!

*   *   *   *   *

Pappy and Grandpap were sowing wheat on the Holloway Ground one cold October afternoon in the late 1940's. There was a pretty good breeze blowing out of the northwest, and once when they stopped to fill the drill they thought they heard someone hollering for help.

They unhooked the drill, then got on the tractor and went looking. South of the house, where the road makes the curve, they discovered a young man stripped to his underpants and tied to a tree at the edge of the road. He was about frozen, and he had been tied so tight for so long that his wrists were red and swollen, and his hands were turning blue.

After they freed him Pappy offered to call the Sheriff, but the boy didn't want any part of that. He was a fraternity pledge and this was part of his initiation. Pappy explained pretty bluntly what his feelings were about a fraternity that would let its members pull crap like that, but the kid wasn't about to rock the boat. They took him to the house and he called someone for a ride, and that was the last we ever heard of him.

*   *   *   *   *

When Grandpap's dad built the log cabin south of Clear Creek and moved to the farm in the early 1860's, he hand dug a well just north of the creek. It was approximately 15' deep and 5' across, was walled up with limestone rocks, and had a 6' square x 8" thick limestone cover, with a square hole chiseled in it large enough for a bucket to go through. Water was usually within 4' of the top. Pappy told me that during the drought of the mid-1930's, neighbors came to the well everyday with wagons full of barrels and hauled water for their livestock.

As more houses were built in the area and more deep wells were drilled, the water table was tapped and by the time Columbia ran their sewer line across the farm in the early 1980's, the water level had dropped to the point that you couldn't sink a bucket in the well.

The sewer ran really close to the well, and after the rock in the ditch had been dynamited I didn't figure the well was very stable anymore, so I asked Ed, the job Foreman, to have his crew cave the well in and fill it. By that time there were so damn many dumbassed trespassers on the farm anyhow, that I was afraid some idiot would leave the well open, then if some kid blundered into it I would be at fault for not doing enough to protect people from their own stupidity. There really should be an open season on trespassers, with no bag limit!

*   *   *   *   *

When I was a little kid, lots of nights after supper I would go to the front of the house with Grandpap, where he and Grandma lived, and he would tell me stories, mostly about things that had happened when he was growing up. One that he told occasionally was about three young men and the neighborhood witch.

Grandpap said that the old woman lived in a little log cabin way off by herself and never mingled with other people. Everyone started saying that she must be a witch. Grandpap told me that one Saturday night three local rowdies had a little too much to drink, and they decided they were going to drag the old woman out of her cabin, give her a "good whuppin'" and chase her out of the neighborhood because they didn't like witches!

They rode their horses to within about 1/4 mile of the cabin, then tied them up to a tree and walked the rest of the way. The cabin had a fireplace with the chimney built on the outside of the house. When they arrived they decided to stand in the "chimney corner" for a few minutes and listen to see if they could tell what the old woman was doing. It just happened that she had three apples baking on the hearth in front of the fireplace. They were getting hot and the skins were starting to crack open, and the apples were going "plup, plup, plup" as they heated. The old woman said "Yeh, yeh, yeh, there's no reason you be a plup, plup, pluppin', 'cause in a minute I'm going to eat all three of you!"

Those three boys looked at each other and one of them asked "was you plup, plup, pluppin'?" The other two shook their heads, and at the same time they all three decided that pluppin' or not, they were getting the hell out of there, before that old witch ate them. The one in front heard the other two running behind him and thought it was the witch, and he ran even faster while the two behind ran faster so they wouldn't get left. By the time they ran through briers and thorns and tripped and fell numerous times, they were pretty messed up when they finally got back to their horses. They made it back to town and then told everyone who would listen how close they had come to being eaten by the witch.

Grandpap always told this as if it was a true story. However, when I got a little older and started questioning him about where this happened and if he had ever seen the old woman, and where did the three boys live and did he know them, he would just smile a little bit of a smile and start telling another story.

*   *   *   *   *

When the hen house on the old place was built in 1939, it was the only building on the farm with a concrete floor.

The first time Pappy and Grandpap cleaned it out, Grandpap got really tired of scraping chicken poop off the floor with a shovel. He picked out a couple of heavy built garden hoes that he didn't use very often, and the next time they were in town they took them to Farmer's Implement Co. and George Sargent heated the hoes in his forge then straightened the hook, turning them into long handled scrapers.

Whoever patented that idea, and called them "spud-hoes," probably made a bunch of money but Grandpap didn't care, he just wanted something to scrape chicken-poop with.

*   *   *   *   *

Previously published in "Farm Collector," used with permission.

When Pappy was growing up Grandpap was still clearing ground on the farm. At that time most farm wages were 50 cents per day. Pappy said that after Grandpap would get an area cut off, he would hire a man who lived in Columbia to grub stumps for 10 cents apiece, regardless of size. Grandpap furnished a team of mules, and all of the necessary tools. Pappy said the man would grub out five small to medium sized stumps to make his day's wages and then he would work for the rest of the day on a really big one. The next day he would switch back to the small and medium stumps 'til he had made 50 cents, then he'd work on the big one again. When he finally got a big stump out, that was an extra 10 cents for the day.

Pappy said when there weren't any stumps to grub the man would split rails for so much per hundred or he would cut and shock corn by the shock, but he wouldn't work for straight wages, because he said "Ain't nobody telling me how damn hard I got to work!"

*   *   *   *   *

Previously published in "Today's Farmer" and "Farm and Ranch Living," used with permission.

Christmas was a lot different in the 1870s than it is today. Times were a lot tougher then, and Old Santa just couldn't afford to make all of the fancy toys that he makes today. Grandpap told me that from the time he could first remember, his Christmas presents always consisted of three or four oranges, a sack of hard candy and maybe a homemade toy. He said he was always "plumb tickled" with these presents, because Christmas was the only time there were ever any oranges in the house and almost the only time he ever got any store-bought candy.

The year that Grandpap turned seven, the family got up on Christmas morning, opened their usual presents, then sat down to eat breakfast. The two-room log cabin they lived in had a rail fence around it, and after they had finished eating Grandpap's Dad told him, "Ed, you ought to go out and look around the fence. Old Santa might have dropped something out of his sack when he was climbing over." Grandpap went out to check and found a beautiful metal horse about eight-inches tall, laying by the fence. It was the first toy he had ever owned that wasn't homemade, and he thought it was the most wonderful thing he had ever seen.

Grandpap played with his horse every chance he got, and he told me, "Cap, the more I played with it the more I got to wondering if my horse had insides, like a real horse." After a couple of weeks, curiosity finally got the better of him, so he took his horse to the barn, got a hammer and chisel and opened it up to find out. "Cap," he said, "the blamed thing was plumb empty, and we never did get my horse where it would stay together again."

Grandpap told me this story one afternoon when he found me in the old buggy house, diligently working on splitting open a toy John Deere tractor with a hammer and chisel. I wanted to see what the engine looked like on the inside. Times change, but kids pretty much stay the same.

*   *   *   *   *

Previously published in "Farm Collector," used with permission.

Pappy was born in 1899. His brother was born in 1901. When they were in their teens, they purchased a stripped-down Ford Model T for $10 and drove the car several years until my uncle got married in 1923. Uncle Edward didn't think that a married man really needed a stripped-down Model T, so he and Pappy traded it even up for a portable buzz saw powered by an eight HP Whitte engine. The saw was on a wagon-type frame with steel wheels and a long tongue, so a team of horses or mules could pull it. Pappy and Uncle Edward sawed wood for their families, several neighbors and anyone else within a ten-mile radius that needed their services.

Pappy told me that at a time when wages were 50 cents a day, they charged $3.50 per day for two men and the saw. Pappy was the sawyer, Uncle Edward would off-bear, and the person they were sawing for furnished enough help to keep wood carried to the saw. They sawed together from 1923 until Uncle Edward quit farming and moved to town in 1941. Even after he moved, Uncle Edward arranged his schedule so he could be at the farm to help on the day Pappy sawed his winter woodpile. Apparently the saw was causing trouble in 1932, because Pappy received some ads for new engines in the mail, along with a parts book and price list. The total cost for the seven needed parts, including a piston, came to $16.80. I don't know if Pappy ordered the parts or not, but I assume he did, since he didn't buy his first tractor until 1939, and something had to power the saw for those seven years in between.

I was born in 1942, and although the engine wasn't in running condition when I was a kid, in my earliest memories the Witte was still loose, and John and Kenny Cavcey and I would play on the old saw for hours. It became a tank, train, airplane, or anything else we wanted it to be. We would turn the large flywheels, causing the piston to open and close with a loud whooshing noise. After we got too old to play with the engine anymore, the piston soon stuck from lack of use.

From a Whitte Engine sales brochure.

From when I can first remember until the early 1970's we sawed our own woodpile and at least two of the neighbors piles each year. By this time the belt pulley on the old 8N Ford tractor powered the saw. Depending on their size, we would either chop trees or cut them down with a crosscut saw then cut off all of the limbs and load them in the wagon and haul them up to the barn lot. We would drag the logs to the lot, and then split them into sections small enough that 3 or 4 men could carry them to the saw. With this much labor involved, old fence posts, scrap lumber and anything else that would make a stick of firewood found its way into the woodpile.

When Pappy finally bought a chain saw in the early '70s, the old buzz saw was retired. In the mid 1970s, the farm joining Pappy's was purchased and developed by Woodhaven Children's Home. One day at noon, a gentleman from the job site showed up at Pappy's door, asking if the old saw was for sale. He had seen it setting by the chicken house, and he wanted to restore it to running condition. The amount of $25 was agreed on, which seemed like a fair

October 1972. Pappy, Mom, and John DeMarce with a big wood pile, some of it still waiting to be sawed. The old saw is partially visible behind Mom.

price. Pappy figured that after 50 years of use, a $15 profit on the original investment wasn't bad. It was a good price at the time, but I do occasionally wonder if it might not be worth a little more today.

I still heat with wood that I cut with a chain saw, but sometimes I think that if the old saw was still around, I'd like to hook up the belt just one more time and show my grandkids what old-fashioned wood sawing was all about.

* * * * *

Grandma was always a fairly heavy woman, but people said that she had pretty legs. I never paid any attention to Grandma's legs, but other people said they were pretty.

Grandma told Sis that after her and Grandpap got married they climbed into a buggy and headed down the road. She said before long Grandpap reached over and pulled her skirt up about halfway to her knees. He took a good long look, let out a big sigh of relief and said, "Thank goodness, I never could abide a woman with thick ankles." Grandma said that she always kind of wondered if she'd had thick ankles what Grandpap intended to do about it, but she never asked.

*   *   *   *   *

Joe Crane told me that when he was a kid his family was starting to get ready for bed one evening when someone noticed that his little brother Jim wasn't there. After a short discussion they realized that Jim hadn't been there at supper time either.

Joe said his parents and the older kids got lanterns and they went looking for Jim. Eventually they discovered him asleep in a manger in the barn. He'd laid down for a nap while the older kids were doing their chores and just kept on sleeping, and no one had missed him 'til bedtime.

Joe said, "We wasn't neglected or nothing like that, but there was just so dad-blamed many of us that it was hard to keep track of everyone all of the time." When you consider the fact that Joe had 13 brothers and sisters, I 'spect he was right.

*   *   *   *   *

Old Joe had a crooked leg. When he worked he wore a heavy brace that fit over his heel and had metal straps that ran up to his knee, and leather straps and buckles that went around his calf and held it tight.

When joe was a little kid he fell out of a tree and broke his leg, and the old country doctor set it crooked. When the cast was removed the doctor looked at the leg and said he'd have to break it again and re-set it. Joe threw a fit, and said, "Ain't nobody breaking my dad-blamed leg again!" No one made him do it, so he had a crooked leg for the rest of his life.

I worked for Joe quite a bit when I was a kid and I never heard him complain about his leg, but I'd almost bet that he wished many times that he'd let that doctor break it again and set it straight.

Back When

Customs sure do change over the years. During the late 1950's and early '60s when Grandma was sick most of the time, Joe Crane would occasionally ride his old mare up to the house to check on Grandma.

If Pappy, Grandpap, or Virginia and I were home he would tie the mare to a tree and come in the house and visit with Grandma for a while. However, if Mom and Grandma were home alone Joe would sit on his horse in the backyard while Mom stood and visited with him for a few minutes, then he would go on his way. Joe was not about to come in the house with two married women when they were home alone. Today, no one would think anything about it.

*   *   *   *   *

Before New Haven School was built I raked a lot of hay for Bill Brynjulfson and his son on Clyde Shepard's farm, in the field where the school and the trailer court are now located. Little Bill's house was about where new Highway 63 is now, and Old Bill's house was just west of where the PetroMart Convenience Store is located. I do believe it looked a lot better back then.

Old Bill had a big 1949 or '50 Mercury that would run like hell. I was 13 or 14 years old and usually when we would go to the house for dinner Bill would toss me the car keys and say, "We're going to drink a couple of beers before dinner, why don't you run up to Walkup's and get yourself some sodas?" I didn't care that much about the sodas; but damn, I did like to drive that Mercury!

*   *   *   *   *

Once when I was a little bitty kid I was running around the yard chasing birds, when Grandpap told me that if I wanted to catch a bird and play with it all I needed to do was sprinkle some salt on its tail. I thought about that for a moment, then asked "When it turns around to peck the salt do I just reach down and grab it?" Grandpap said, "Just sprinkle the salt, then you'll figure it out from there."

I wandered around half the summer with a pocket full of damp, sweaty salt. I finally told Grandpap that there just wasn't any way I could get close enough to a bird to sprinkle salt on its tail. He said "Well Cap, that's where you usually kinda run into a problem. I reckon that's why you don't see very many people playing with birds."

*   *   *   *   *

Fred and Kathi Vom Saal were as good of neighbors as Mom could have asked for when she lived alone on the farm, and they have continued to be good neighbors over the years.

Several years ago they bought 10 acres off the old Joe Crane Place, that someone else had already built a house on. The first owner wasn't quite as good a neighbor as Fred and Kathi. Matter of fact, he didn't like me a damn bit. The first time I met him I was working on the old fence that ran between his yard and Mom's farm, when he walked out of his house and started visiting. After introducing himself he said, "We certainly hope you don't intend to ever do anything with that beautiful piece of ground, because we want it to stay green space forever."

I looked at him and said "Yeah, that's how I always felt about your place, before you bought it and built that damn house on it."

I guess that remark offended him because he lived there for several years before he sold the place to Fred and Kathi and he never spoke to me again.

*   *   *   *   *

John Brown worked maintenance at Woodhaven Home for several years (Not John Brown the pipe fitter). After Pappy passed away in 1982, Mom made arrangements with John for him to mow her yard. There was plenty of time for him to mow it after he got off work in the afternoon, so it worked out good for both of them.

One spring when John came for the first time he and Mom visited for a few minutes, then he asked, "Mrs. Easley, how do you like my new tooth?" John smiled a big old smile and right in front, shining like a diamond in a goat's ass, was a solid gold tooth. Mom said, "Well John that's a nice tooth, but I thought you had dentures." John replied, "I do, but I always wanted a gold tooth so I took them to the dentist and told him to put one in."

*   *   *   *   *

There is a beautiful old pie safe in our family room that we've had almost ever since we built our house in 1963. Marcia and I went north of town to a Jacobs and Kemper farm auction one afternoon back in the 1960's, and ran across an old pie safe with no telling how many coats of various colored paint on it.

That was back when a dollar was a dollar, furniture was cheap, and bids were small. Bandy started the safe for a couple of bucks, and I ran it all the way up to $7.00. Someone else bid $7.25, and when Bandy asked me for

Marcia and me, 1961

$7.50 I shook my head no and walked away. I hadn't gotten very far when I heard Bandy say "Sold, Easley, $7.50." I turned around and told Bandy I didn't bid $7.50. He grinned from ear to ear, pointed at Marcia, and said "By God, she did!" My baby wasn't about to lose that pie safe over 25 cents. We hauled it home, she stripped it and refinished it, and we've used it ever since. Babe, I'm glad you spent that extra quarter.

*   *   *   *   *

Back when I was still in grade school a young man knocked on our door one cold night around 11:30. He told us he was an M.U. student, and he was so nervous he couldn't hardly talk. He was parked up the road north of Cavcey's with a Stephens' girl; at that time the curfew for Stephens' girls was 12:00 midnight and the school did just about everything except execute them if they were late. They'd been running the heater and the engine got hot, so he shut it off to let it cool down. It wouldn't re-start and he said he needed a bucket of water, and he wanted us to pull-start his car.

Pappy didn't want to get out at that time of night, so I got dressed and pumped a bucket of water from the cistern, then we headed up the road on the tractor with the guy standing on the draw bar holding on with one hand and holding that sloshing bucket of water in the other hand. When we got to the car he poured the water in the radiator while I hooked up the chain, then he set the empty bucket in the car so it would be out of the way. I pulled his car and got it started and as soon as I unhooked the chain he backed up and cut around the tractor, then headed up the road with gravel flying. I used every word I knew as I stood there shaking my fist at his tail lights and calling him a no good sorry-assed bucket stealing worthless son-of-a-bitch! Besides losing the bucket, I'd expected to get 2 or 3 dollars out of the deal, and I was really pissed about not getting my money.

For the next 2 or 3 days every time I'd think about that deal, I'd cuss that sorry bastard again. One afternoon I got off the school bus, and setting in the middle of the driveway was the bucket with a five-dollar bill in the bottom weighted down with a rock. I don't know if he decided to do that on his own, or if his girlfriend convinced him that he should, but either way he didn't have enough balls to talk to anyone, but at least we did get our bucket back. And I made five bucks, damn near a winter's wages for a 12-year-old kid back in the 1950's.

*   *   *   *   *

When I was a kid our bath water had to be pumped out of the cistern or hauled in a barrel from the old well down by the creek, and then heated in a big pot on the wood stove. I guess that's why we shared bath water in the winter. I never did like to take a bath in used water, but it beat no bath at all.

In the summer, me, Grandpap, and Pappy would take a bar of soap and some towels and walk down to the creek for a bath. By the time we walked back up the hill, with dust puffing up around our feet with every step we had worked up a pretty good sweat, but at least it was fresh dust and fresh sweat. However, I never did figure out why we didn't take the tractor and wagon down to the creek when we took baths, at least that way we would have still been clean when we got back to the house.

*   *   *   *   *

When I first got my driver's license, Pappy had a light green 1951 Chevy and Vencil Sapp had a light blue 1955 Ford. Whenever Elra and I would meet each other, we'd swap sides of the road and pass without slowing down.

One day I was headed north on Range Line Road when I spotted Elra (I thought) in the blue Ford. I moved to the left and kept driving. The Ford kept coming in its own lane, then finally stopped. I pulled back onto my side of the road and stopped when I got alongside the Ford. I then proceeded to get one hell of a good ass-chewing from Vencil, he was not impressed with that little caper. I guaran-damn-tee that the next time I saw that blue Ford I got close enough to identify the driver before I pulled to the wrong side of the road.

*   *   *   *   *

One year when I was on the Board of Directors at Boone Co. Oil Co-op we were in the process of buying a new refined fuels delivery truck. Carl Triplett told me that he had mentioned to Dale Pipes (Co-op Manager) that an air-ride seat would really be nice, but Dale told him they were too expensive.

At our next Board meeting I asked Dale what he thought about putting an air-ride seat in the new truck. He replied, "Oh hell no, they cost $400.00, we're not spending that much on a truck seat." I said "Dale, that chair in your office probably cost $400.00, and all you do is sit on your ass in front of your desk. These guys spend 8 or 10 hours a day bouncing around on some of the worst roads in Boone County. If an air-ride seat will make their lives more pleasant, I don't have a problem with that."

The Board pretty much agreed, so the next day Dale called and added an air-ride seat to the spec sheet for the new truck. Dale didn't like it, but Carl got his air-ride seat, and as far as I can remember we put an air-ride seat in every truck we bought after that.

*   *   *   *   *

My cousin Burdette Cheavens told me that when he was Chief of Police in Columbia, Earl Crane did as much to keep the peace as anyone on the force.

At that time the Patrol officers all carried a 4-battery flashlight. Burdette said as far as he knew Earl never had to draw his gun, but he did go through a lot of flashlights.

One night there was a knife fight down at Sharp-end, so Earl went to settle things down. When he got back to the Station Burdette asked him if he had any trouble. Earl said "No not really, I had to send a couple of the boys to the hospital for stitches, but the rest of them were pretty agreeable. I am going to need another flashlight, though." He tossed his old one on the desk, and Burdette said it was almost "L" shaped, and the big end was covered with dried blood and hair. Today some do-good son-of-a-bitch would holler police brutality, but Columbia sure was more peaceful back then than it is now.

*   *   *   *   *

Sis told me that when she was in High School, Mom looked at her one day and said "Virginia, I'm really sorry that you inherited that short, dumpy Cheavens body." Sis replied, "Well thank you for the ego booster, Mom, you're not that tall yourself."

*   *   *   *   *

Several years ago at a family reunion, my cousin Esther overheard several of us discussing guns. After our conversation was over she came up to me and said "Alan, I heard you talking about guns a while ago, I've got a gun that Dad made, would you like to have it?" Would I like to have it? I RECKON! She explained all that she knew about the gun, and I suggested that it would probably be best to bury the gun in the trunk of their car and bring it to Missouri that way, rather than mailing it.

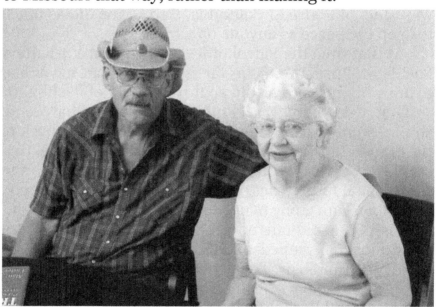

Cousins. Esther Thames and me at a family reunion, July 2013.

Two or three years later at a reunion Esther said that she had the gun in their car. When she gave it to me I immediately checked it out. It was a sawed off, single shot bolt action rifle, with homemade grips and a handmade brass trigger and trigger guard. The gun showed some pretty good workmanship. When I thanked her for the gun she said she was glad I took it because none of their kids wanted it, and she and Stan didn't want to throw it away. As soon as I got home I tried it out. It's not really very accurate, but at 15' you can hit a paper plate nearly every time.

A couple of years later I was talking to Esther's brother, Frank. Somehow the conversation finally made it around to the subject of guns, and Frank said "You know, when I was 16 or 17 years old Dad cut a tree down on his rifle one day and bent the barrel. I took his gun to shop class at Hickman High School, sawed off that bent barrel, dove tailed the shortened barrel and re-installed the sight, made pistol grips, a trigger and trigger guard, and pretty soon I had a functioning gun. That old thing was around for years, but I don't have any idea what ever became of it." I kinda grinned and said, "Hell Frank, I know what became of it, your sister gave it to me a couple of years ago, you want it back?" Frank told me to keep it because he didn't have any use for it, he was just glad to find out what had finally happened to it.

Times sure do change. Can you imagine the amount of shit that would hit the fan today if a 16-year-old kid carried a crooked barreled rifle into shop class and told the teacher that he was going to build a pistol? Hell, the kid would be in jail, suspended for at least the rest of the year, and the whole school would be on lockdown for a week while the bomb squad hunted for more guns. Life sure was simpler back then.

*   *   *   *   *

Twenty years or so ago, the county decided that they needed to replace the bridge on Bearfield Road. There was no question that it needed to be replaced, but the county had some highly-educated idiot-assed engineer working for them, who decided that three culvert pipes would be lots cheaper than a bridge. I'd been around

Clear Creek all of my life, and I knew that wasn't going to work, so I sent a letter to the Public Works Department expressing my concerns. Mr. Big-shit engineer quickly decided that no dumb-assed farmer was going to tell him what would or wouldn't work. There were several letters and phone calls back and forth over the next month, and I finally received a letter stating that "our engineer has assured us that the culverts will handle 10 gallons per minute more water than will ever come down that creek." BULLSHIT!

Before long the bridge was removed and replaced with three culverts. During construction the Public Works Director told me that if they could remove my water gap it would make it easier for them, and they would replace it when they were finished. I should have gotten that in writing because the son-of-a-bitches don't remember anything about that now. After the culverts were installed, the county cut three circles out of cattle panels that would fit inside of the culverts, and hung each of them with two strands of #9 wire. Hot damn, no way in hell that could possibly plug up or wash out in a big rain!

The first time the creek got up a little, it more than took care of that 10 gallon per minute crap. The cattle panels were plugged with leaves and small limbs, an 18" tree trunk about 15' long was lodged crossways in front of the culverts, and several big limbs were tangled in front of them. I was 50 some years old at the time and I'd never seen water over Bearfield Road, however, the first time that the creek went on a boom after that it put 2' of water over the road for about 300 yards. The county had to barricade the road to keep someone from driving into the water and floating away.

That same dumb-assed engineer that designed the culverts quickly solved the problem of water over the road. The county raised the road 30" for about 400 yards, but of course after they did that I couldn't get off the road and go through my gate into the field so they had to rebuild my access. I 'spect that the cost of installing the culverts, raising the road, and rebuilding my access would have just about paid for a new bridge, but they'll never admit it, they've got to cover their asses.

Those circles of cattle panel washed away years ago, but there's always enough drift in front of the culverts to keep cattle from walking into them. It's a good thing because the uncooperative asshole who is in charge of the road shed now says he doesn't know anything about a water gap, that was before his time. If you have to deal with the Boone County Government, get it in writing because a hand shake agreement will just wind up getting you a really good screwing.

*   *   *   *   *

When I was 10 or 12 years old I read every "Hardy Boys" book that was ever published. I would save my pennies and nickels, and when we would go to town on Saturday I'd go to the bookstore and pay 75 cents for the latest copy. On the cover of one of the books was a picture of Joe Hardy wearing a black and white checked short sleeve shirt. At that time Mom made all of my shirts out of feed sacks. One day we were at Boone County Feed Company and right on the bottom of a stack of feed were two black and white checked sacks. Poor Uncle Edward, who was part owner of the feed store at the time, had to move all of those 100 lb. sacks to get to my shirt material.

Mom kept checking the picture on the book when she made that shirt, to be sure the pockets, collar, and everything else matched perfectly. I was so proud of my "Hardy Boys" shirt that I didn't know what to do. I wore it every time it was clean until there wasn't anything left of it. When that shirt finally came out of the washing machine for the last time it wouldn't have even made a good dust rag.

If you run into Paul McAtee sometime, ask about his mom making feed sack shirts for him. I wasn't the only one who wore them.

*   *   *   *   *

When James Earl Grant was hauling lime, back before he and Dorothy got married, he pulled in C.J. Tekotte's driveway one morning with a load of lime and stopped to find out where he was going to spread. Jay came out of the house and immediately dropped to his hands and knees and started crawling towards James Earl's truck, hollering "Get down, Grant, get down!" James Earl looked around, then asked Jay what the hell was going on. Tekotte replied "Hell Grant, you're running Estes' daughter and he's standing out at his barn with a gun, get down before he shoots your ass!" There was never a dull moment when that old man was alive, he kept the pot stirred at all times.

*   *   *   *   *

The first time Bill Gentzsch met Ruth he was standing in Tekotte's driveway talking to Jay when she came out of the house. Jay said "Boy, take a good look at her. Every man ought to marry a fat woman like her, they keep you warm in the winter and make a hell of a lot of shade in the summertime." It didn't bother Ruth, she was used to it, but it embarrassed the hell out of Bill.

*   *   *   *   *

After Marcia and I got married in 1961 and started raising a family I settled down quite a bit, and didn't give Pappy quite as many reasons to get upset as I did when I was a little younger. However, I still dropped one on him occasionally. One summer Pappy and Mom were hosts to a large family reunion, with guests ranging in age from diapers to ninety. After the usual big carry-in dinner everyone settled down for a quiet afternoon. The young kids were playing, some of the older guests were dozing in their chairs, and several small groups had splintered off and were having quiet or spirited conversations, depending on the group.

Pappy had recently purchased a new .32 caliber revolver, and as we often did when several of us got together, we wound up in the barn lot target shooting. Pappy always stacked his firewood in the center of the lot, and over the years there is no telling how many shots were fired into the wood pile.

We set up some tin cans in front of the pile, and had probably been shooting for thirty minutes or so when Little Sarah's husband decided to try something a little different. He was a policeman in St. Louis, and therefore, shot a pistol a lot more than the rest of us, and he wanted to show us how he could shoot from the hip; he wasn't too bad, he hit several cans and got close enough to the rest of them to make them jump. After several shots he asked us if anyone else wanted to try it. I'd never shot from the hip before, but I was pretty cocky back then, and I figured if a St. Louis slicker could do it, I could too. I loaded the gun and shot one time, and couldn't even tell where the bullet hit. Someone said that I had shot too high, so I pulled down a little and shot again. I still couldn't tell anything, but I was told that I was still shooting too high. I pulled down some more and shot again and we immediately heard a "splot," and a hole appeared in the tin roof of the barn which was on the other side of the wood pile.

No one said anything for a moment, and Pappy just stood there looking at the hole in the roof, then looking at me, then back at the hole. I knew it was coming, and it finally did. Pappy looked back at me again, shook his head, then said; "GOOD GOSH-A-MIGHTY, ALAN."

The old barn was almost one hundred years old at the time, and not in very good condition, so Pappy decided that he'd rather have a hole in the roof than to have me fall off the barn if I tried to fix it. That was close to 50 years ago, but the barn is still standing, (just barely) and if you walk up to it today and know where to look you can still see that bullet hole in the roof.

*   *   *   *   *

Previously published in "Looking Back." Used with permission.

By the time I was old enough to work in the hayfield Pappy and Grandpap were getting a neighbor, Curt Stone, to bale their hay with a mule powered stationary baler. However, Charlie Hall still loose-stacked all of his hay. Charlie mowed with a horse drawn mower, raked with a horse drawn sulky rake, then pushed the hay to the stack with a long-tom rake, using the same two horses. I often wondered if that old team didn't get tired of seeing the same field every day.

The summer that I turned 12 years old, Charlie announced to everyone in the neighborhood that I was going to learn how to stack hay. The day we started he pushed up several rakes full, explained to me how to build the base of the stack, then went back to raking while Tom Watson pitched to me. I'd never stacked hay before, but Charlie must have done a pretty good job of teaching me, because none of the stacks that I built over a three or four-year period ever fell down.

I never heard Charlie say a cuss word in his life, but when he called you a "pot-licking old hound," you knew he was getting just a little bit upset. I was a "pot-licker" on a fairly regular basis when I was building the first two or three stacks. I can still hear Charlie today; "GET out there and stomp that edge, you pot-licker, you won't fall off, if you do you can climb back up. GET out there!" I never cared much for climbing trees when I was a kid because they grew too far from the ground to suit me, and the higher those hay stacks got the more trouble Charlie had getting me to stomp the edges. I felt a lot safer when I was in the middle of the stack, but with Charlie urging me on I somehow managed to keep the edges pretty well stomped.

In the mid 1960's Charlie sold his farm to the Missouri Rock Bridge State Park and I hadn't been on the place from that time until the summer of 2000. I walked into the park one day looking for the old hay field and I had trouble finding it. The timothy and lespedeza had turned into thorn trees, persimmon sprouts, and cedar trees big enough to make good fence posts. I liked it a lot better when it was a hayfield.

*   *   *   *   *

When my nephew, Karl DeMarce, stayed with Momma while he was attending MU back in the 1980's, the old house was really beginning to need a new roof. The original part of the house had wood shingles with 3 layers of asphalt shingles over them. The first addition had wood shingles with 2 layers of asphalt, and the kitchen had 1 layer of asphalt shingles, standing rib metal, then roll roofing had been applied over the metal, because of a leak no one could locate. Mom got 3 bids from roofing contractors and they were all plumb out of sight because of the labor involved. None of them would even consider installing a new roof without first removing all of the old material down to the rafters, and then completely sheeting it because all that it had was strips to nail the wood shingles onto.

J.C. Rupard lived in the little house on the Schwabe Farm at that time, and he was pretty much a "Jack-of-all-trades." J.C. looked at the old house, then said if he could buy roofing nails that were long enough he would put a new roof over what was there. He located some 4" nails, and shingled the old house for less than a third of what the other bids were. It's a good thing that the roof has a steep pitch because 5 layers is a hell of a lot of weight on those 145-year-old 2"x4" oak rafters.

When Mom told Karl what she was going to do he couldn't hardly believe it. He asked "Grandma, why don't you do it right while you're doing it?" Mom looked at him and with that slow New York accent she said "Karl, this will last me as long as I need a roof. After I'm dead if someone wants to do it right, that's their privilege." Mom died in 2006, and that roof sure 'nuff lasted as long as she needed it, and it still doesn't leak. There are a hell of a lot of other things on the old house that are about used up, but that roof is still good after nearly 30 years.

*   *   *   *   *

Previously published in "The Ozark's Mountaineer," used with permission.

The year I was a sophomore in high school I was only 15 years old, but one of my classmates, Cornbread Heath, was 16 and had a driver's license. It was a great year for lespedeza and there was a lot of hay baled after school started in the fall. Cornbread's older brother, Mel, had a 3/4 ton Chevy truck with a flat bed and Cornbread rented it from him for 2 cents per bale, and we went into the hay hauling business after school, charging 12 cents per bale. We did several jobs, hauling 300 to 400 bales per night, and thought we had found a sure way to wealth.

One morning before school, Cornbread told me he had lined up an 800-bale job. Neither of us knew the man we were going to haul for, but that didn't really matter; we thought hay was hay. We arrived at the farm after school and the elderly owner (He looked elderly to us, but he was probably several years younger than I am now) informed us that he would have to lead us to the field, because we couldn't find it by ourselves. He got on his tractor and headed across a pasture, threading his way between cedar trees and thorn sprouts.

I thought I was raised in the hills, but I'd never seen hills like these. We went straight down the first one because it was too steep to drive on crossways. At the bottom of the hill we made a very rough creek crossing, drove across a small bottom, crossed a deep ditch and finally arrived at the field. By this time we were beginning to have our doubts about ever getting back with a load of hay, but we were willing to try anything, at least once. Like I said, we thought hay was hay and I guess it was, but damn few people can squeeze as much hay into a bale as this guy had. The light ones weighed at least 90 lbs. and they went rapidly upwards from there. We finally got loaded, tied the load down and headed back towards civilization.

We made it across the ditch and almost made it across the creek. After wading about 6" of water to reload a half dozen very wet and very heavy bales, we retied the load and started up the hill. About half way up our old rotten rope broke, and several bales rolled off the truck. DAMN IT! Oh well, not fun but no big deal; reload, splice the rope, retie and go again. The only problem was, the hill was so steep that when Cornbread let the clutch out the front of the truck came off the ground. He clutched, then tried it again. This time the front end stayed down because the rope broke again and about half the load tumbled off the back. There wasn't enough rope left to splice again so we turned around, reloaded and tried to back up the hill.

By then it was dark, so Cornbread was hanging out the door with a flashlight watching for cedar trees, and I was holding the gearshift since the old truck had an annoying habit of jumping out of reverse. Even with me holding the gearshift it jumped out about every 20 feet or so. Before Cornbread could hit the brakes we would roll back down the hill about 10 feet. We finally gave up and walked to the house to see if we could borrow a tractor to pull the truck up the hill.

The old gentleman told us that wouldn't be necessary because there was a shed on the other side of the creek. We got in his old pickup with him and headed back down the hill. We decided to leave our truck where it was and get it on the way back. By this time the old fella had been in the beer bucket pretty hard, and we were kinda glad he was driving in the field instead of on the road. We crossed the creek, the ditch and the hay field, drove about 200 yards on a path cut through a patch of woods, then came out of the woods into a field of horse weeds at least 10' tall, and headed towards the shed. Or so we thought! It was a really dark night and all we could see in the headlights were horse weeds. After a little while the old fella stopped, looked around, mumbled "Humph" and started driving again. He soon turned around, moved over a little ways and headed back. After a couple of more tries he stopped, looked around again and said "Dammit, boys, I know the damn thing is still standing because I saw it last spring. It don't matter, it's too damn late to start hauling hay anyway." He told us to unload what we had on the truck right where it was, then said "It ain't gonna rain, I'll find that damn shed when it gets daylight, and you can haul the damn hay tomorrow evening." I'd never heard so many "damns" strung together in two sentences in all my life.

We returned the next day after school with a new rope and two extra bodies, and spent most of the night getting over 800 very heavy bales of hay safely stashed away in a raggedy-assed old shed. We did several more small jobs before hay season was over, but after that experience we checked them out a lot closer before we committed ourselves.

*   *   *   *   *

Previously published in "Successful Farming," used with permission.

When Marcia and I got married in 1961, we rented the little house at Wat and Thelma Cheavens' Place south of Pierpont for a couple of years. From the day of the wedding we were pretty sure we would be "chivareed."

To get us in the mood for a chivaree, visitors made sure our bed collapsed the second night we were home from our Honeymoon. The slats had been sawed almost through. The next morning when I left the house Wat was out in his yard. We exchanged greetings, then he asked how we were doing. I replied, "Not worth a damn, my back's sore, we had to spend the night on the floor, our bed collapsed."

Wat didn't say a word, he just turned and walked into his garage. He soon came back out with a big smile on his face and a bundle of 1"x4"'s on his shoulder. He said, "Some of your friends stopped by and left these with me last week. They said they're already cut to fit, and they thought you'd probably be needing them."

From then on every evening I hid our car in Wat's barn, and made a point of locking the front door. The little house didn't have a back door. The door didn't fit real good, and I had to kick the bottom of it, and then bump it with my knee to make sure the lock had fully engaged. After a couple of weeks we started thinking we had lucked out, and we got a little careless. I quit hiding the car, and occasionally Marcia would lock the door. On the night of the chivaree she locked it, but she didn't kick it quite hard enough.

About 1:00 a.m. we heard several shotgun blasts just outside our bedroom window, and at the same time the front door popped open and soon several people crowded into our bedroom. Marcia's little brother, Bob, wanted to pull the sheet off, but thank God Forrest Cowden convinced him that wasn't really a good idea. After we got presentable we went into the living room to visit with the group of people who were crowded in there. Between the living room and the front yard we were hosts to 40 or 50 friends and family members, and a few people whom we didn't even know. Someone just invited them to come along and join in the fun. Everyone was drinking beer or soda pop and eating snacks. They had been afraid we wouldn't have enough refreshments on hand, so before they came to the house they went by Tee-Pee Town, a local liquor store, and convinced the owner, Chub Armstrong, to charge the refreshments to me. It cost me $35.00. At the time I was only making $45.00 per week.

Elra Sapp brought an iron wheeled wheel barrow along, and they had me take Marcia for a ride down the gravel driveway. When that was finished they decided to throw me in a nearby pond. I was making it rough enough on them that they stopped at a watering tank and dumped me in it instead because it was a hell of a lot closer, but I still got soaked. While we were outside, some of our dear friends and relatives were keeping busy removing the labels from all of our canned goods, and dumping salt, pepper and cracker crumbs in our bed.

Around 3:30 a.m. everyone told us what a good time they'd had, wished us a good life, and left us with the mess. But I guaran-damn-tee, over the next few years we returned the favor to several of the participants.

*   *   *   *   *

Previously published in "The Cattleman's Advocate," used with permission.

Several years ago, while Jeff and I were rehanging some gates in the loading pens at the old farm on Bearfield Road, I started thinking about when I was a kid, growing up on this same farm. Sis and I, Pappy and Momma, and Grandpap and Grandma all shared the same old house where Jeff lives now. Most of my time was spent fishing, playing with John Cavcey, going to the field with Pappy, or tagging along with Grandpap as he worked on one of his numerous projects.

It seemed like Grandpap was always in the process of building or repairing at least one gate. In bad weather the gate would be set on saw horses in the old buggy house, in good weather it would be on saw horses under the big walnut tree in the corner of the barn lot. The gates were all built out of wood, either white oak or walnut, sawed out of logs that had been cut on the farm. Nearly all of the gates were bolted together, but there were a few that had been built when a gate was needed in a hurry that were fastened with clenched nails, but the nailed gates tended to loosen up and sag a lot worse than the bolted gates. We didn't know what power tools were back then, so all the slats were cut to length with a handsaw, and all of the bolt holes were drilled with a brace and bit.

Grandpap was in his upper 80's at the time, and I was only eight to ten years old, but I was pretty damn sure that I knew more about building and fixing gates than he did. Grandpap would tell me how he intended to do a certain project, and then I would proceed to tell him how he should do it. We would argue back and forth for a while, then he would say in a disgusted tone of voice, "All right Cap, all right, have it your way." Then he would proceed to do it the way he had intended to in the first place. I always won the arguments, but I don't remember that we ever fixed a gate the way I thought it should have been done.

However, if Grandpap could see the barn lot today he would realize that I was learning a little something as I went along, even if we didn't usually agree.

*   *   *   *   *

I ran into Ray and Doris Crowley at Walmart in February 2014, and we blocked the aisle for 30 minutes or more while we stood there and dredged up lots of old square dance memories. Marcia and I danced with the Centralia "Star Promenaders" a bunch of times back in the late 1960's and 1970's when Ray was their caller:

Eddie (Babe) Gross called for our club in Columbia, the "Dudes and Dames," and Whimpe Phillipe and Bob Schultz called for the other two Columbia Clubs. After Babe Gross retired, Herbie Aholt started calling for the Dudes and Dames.

Two good callers, Whimpy Phillipe and Ray Crowley.

We also danced in Fulton, Jefferson City, Eldon, Rolla, Boonville, Fayette, and occasionally Moberly, Bell Flower, Sedalia and most anywhere else, if someone heard there was going to be a dance. There were a lot of good callers around central Missouri at that time, and some not so good, but except for the ones I've already mentioned, their names have gotten away from me over the years.

Bob and Linda Schultz had a big old Mercury station wagon that would hold at least five couples, and when Marcia and I, Gary and Lynn Chandler, and whoever else happened to be going along climbed into that thing with them to go to a dance we knew we were in for a hell of a ride. Bob didn't know what slow meant, but somehow we always made it back in one piece.

Ray said that if you want to dance today you really have to hunt for somewhere to go, because most of the clubs have folded up over the years. Everything runs in cycles, and right now square dancing has sort of bottomed out, but we had a hell of a lot of fun for quite a few years.

*　　*　　*　　*　　*

Years ago, there was a lot of business conducted by handshake. Back when Marcia and I were square dancing every weekend people were always making deals at the dances. If you needed to order some tractor parts, or maybe finalize a tractor trade, Henry and Anita Semon would be there, Wayne and Margaret Vandeloecht or Donnie and Linda Vandeloecht, and sometimes all these couples on the same night.

If you needed a barn or garage built Lewis and Janice Baumgartner were usually there. Around 1970 I purchased the red barn that is located on the hill west of my house at a dance one night in December. Lewis and I sat down between sets, sized the barn and agreed on a price, then shook hands on the deal. No money was involved, just the handshake. It was April before Lewis got around to starting on my barn. The afternoon that he came by to stake it out he told me that I'd saved some money by ordering it in December, because identical barns had gone up $500.00 over the winter. I don't need the barn nearly as bad as I used to, but it has a bunch of hay in it for Leah's horses, and a pile of old oak lumber that we salvaged from the big barn on Bearfield Road, so it's not going to waste. But the roof's starting to need paint pretty bad, where the hell are you at, Jimmy Riley?

*   *   *   *   *

Grandpap was never real free with his compliments. Once when I was a little bitty kid the whole family was in the old '37 Chevy, making our weekly trip to town.

As Pappy drove through the Stephens College area he and Grandpap were commenting on what nice shapes the Stephens girls had. Sis listened for a little bit, then asked, "Grandpap, do you think Grandma has a nice shape?" He replied, "Oh, it does very well, I reckon."

*   *   *   *   *

When Grandpap was growing up during the 1870's and early 1880's, women pretty much wore their skirts dragging the ground and he never got used to the change in styles.

He thought if women were wearing shorts, or skirts that weren't at least mid-calf, it was pretty much scandalous. He'd tell me, "Cap, they're just about showing you all they've got, and then they wonder why stuff happens." He'd continue, "Why when I was a boy we'd hang around the foot of the stairs when the girls were walking up and down, and if we got real lucky we'd get a glimpse of an ankle occasionally." Then he'd shake his head and say, "Now look at 'em, Cap, huh, huh, huh."

I'd look at them, and I thought they looked pretty damn good, but Grandpap never did get used to all of that skin showing.

*   *   *   *   *

In my first book I mentioned the auction that Pappy and Mom had in September 1976, when they sold stuff that had accumulated on the farm over the past 130-some years. Guess what? I found some pictures. Some of it was pretty neat old stuff.

*   *   *   *   *

Previously published in "Farm Collector," used with permission.

When I was a kid Pappy always wore a winter cap with ear-flaps during real cold weather, but the rest of the year he just made do with whatever he had available. Spring and fall it would usually be an old felt dress hat that had gotten a little bit too shabby for dress-up use. If his head started getting hot he would take scissors and snip a series of holes around the crown of the hat for ventilation. During the summer he usually had an old straw hat that he wore. It was never a wide-brimmed "farmer" hat, he always wore a demoted dress hat.

From the time I was first able to hold on until I got big enough to drive a tractor myself, whatever Pappy happened to be doing I rode on the tractor with him. He had an 8N Ford and I would stand on the step-plate, lean against the fender and hold on with both hands. One summer I was riding while Pappy was cutting wheat with the 8N and a five-foot Case combine. He was wearing an extra raggedy old straw hat that summer, and one day he said, "Alan, this old hat is about used up, when we get done cutting wheat I'm going to throw it in the combine."

The day we got finished he let the combine run until it was pretty well cleaned out, then he tossed that old hat into the header. We watched while it rode up the canvas and disappeared into the cylinder. Pappy pulled up a few feet and took the PTO out of gear, then we walked around behind the combine to see how many pieces of the hat we could find.

We found one. The hat was mashed flat, but other than that it was un-hurt. Pappy picked it up and slapped it against his leg to knock the dust off, punched it back into shape and put it back on his head. "I don't believe it was quite as used up as I thought," he remarked. The best I can remember, Pappy wore that old hat for the rest of the summer.

*   *   *   *   *

Back in the 1940's Jap Willingham and his family moved to the farm on Gans Road that is now owned by Jim and Tom Watson.

Mr. Willingham just had one ear, the other one had been bitten off in a fight. Beatrice Judd Bradshaw told me that the best she can remember, a man by the name of McMillan bit it off at an open-air dance that was held on the Rock Bridge farm, where the State Park is now.

I was a little bitty kid when they moved in, and the first time we were going to be somewhere where the Willinghams' would be, Mom cornered me and said "Alan, Mr. Willingham just has one ear, whatever you do don't you dare stare at his missing ear." Damn, that was just about the same as giving me a license to stare! If she hadn't said anything I would have probably glanced at him, realized that he had an ear missing and then gone on about my business; We attended Little Bonne Femme Church when I was a kid and Charlie Trimble, a member of the congregation, had gold teeth but I didn't stare at him, the old man had gold teeth, it wasn't really a big deal. And Gladys Pauley had club feet but I didn't stare at her. She walked a little slower than most people and her feet were shaped different, but it wasn't anything to stare at. But when Momma told me not to stare at Mr. Willingham's missing ear, that made it a WHOLE different deal.

Jap's ear lobe was still there, and he had two vertical grooves in the side of his head where McMillan's upper teeth had gouged in pretty deep. I thought it was the most interesting looking thing I had ever seen in my whole life, and I spent as much time looking at it as possible. I don't remember how long the Willinghams' lived on Gans Road, but I do remember that I was still "Not Staring" at the missing ear every time I got a chance, right up 'til the day that they moved away.

Cuttin' Cats

When I was a kid, we always had an ass-pocket full of barn cats. They got a pan-full of milk morning and evening, and other than that they were pretty much on their own. Sis always had a few of them gentled down, but most of them were just there.

One big old yellow and white tom was always getting torn up in a cat fight somewhere. One morning while we were milking we kept hearing a cat yowling. We finally spotted the old cat coming slowly up the lane from the road. One of his nuts was dragging the ground between his hind legs, and the other one was swinging free and bobbing up and down when he walked. Every time he took a step he squalled. He had been in a fight, and the other cat's claws had effectively castrated him. He was one unhappy cat! Pappy sprayed him with disinfectant, and in a few days his now useless nuts dried up and dropped off. It did a pretty good job of turning him into a big old fat stay at home cat.

$*$ $*$ $*$ $*$ $*$

One morning when Doris Blackwell started her car to go to work, she immediately heard a whomping noise and then a cat squalled and came out from under the engine compartment. Their big yellow tomcat that Jo Behymer had given Vickie when it was just a kitten headed towards the barn with fur flying.

When Doris got home that evening, the old cat was curled up on the carport, minus his nuts and part of his tail. The fan blades had done as slick a job of castrating that cat as it's possible to do. Her cat lived to be twenty years old, and he got so fat he couldn't hardly walk. The only time he even got off the carport was when he had to go the bathroom. He'd have probably been killed in a cat fight a long time before he actually died, if Doris hadn't performed that accidental surgery.

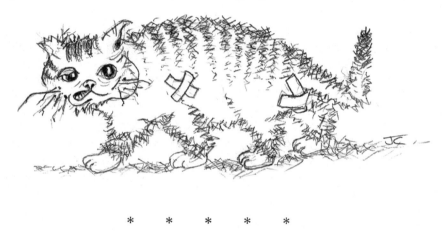

*   *   *   *   *

When our boys were fairly young they had a black tomcat who had turned into quite a roamer. He would drag himself home pretty well chewed and clawed from a cat fight, then he would lay around recovering for 2 or 3 weeks before heading out to do it all over again.

One Saturday James Earl Grant and Larry McCray had helped me vaccinate and castrate a bunch of calves. As usual Larry was the knife man. After we finished we walked to the house to see if we might accidently find some cold beer. The garage door was open, and when we walked in Larry saw the old cat and commented on his chewed-up ears. I said, "Hell, Larry, as much as he roams around, it's a wonder he has any ears left." Larry said, "Hold him and I'll cut him. That'll calm him down."

That sounded like a good idea to me. I'd always heard if you want to cut a tomcat stuff him headfirst into a boot, so that's what I tried to do. I guaran-damn-tee you have to be a lot tougher than I was to stuff a tomcat into a boot. He didn't want any part of that boot and he damn near ate me alive. I turned him loose and after he calmed down a little I said, "Nice kitty," and while I was petting him, I suddenly rolled him up in a heavy hooded sweatshirt with just his nuts and tail sticking out. I laid him on the workbench and stuck my elbow where I thought his neck was, and applied pressure until he started gurgling. Larry put the knife to him, and then sprayed him with disinfectant.

I told the boys to get back, because I figured the old cat would probably go crazy when I turned him loose, but he didn't. I dumped him on the floor and unrolled the shirt, fully expecting him to start bouncing off the walls. Instead, he yowled and twitched his tail a couple of times, then sat down on that cool concrete floor and drug his butt for about six feet, and then he just laid down and curled up. The old cat recovered with no problems, and I don't think he ever left our yard again after that.

Workin' Cattle

At one time Inez Hickam and I seemed to be running a contest to see who had the worst handling cattle. Mine were wild and crazy and some of them were mean, but Inez's cattle were wild and crazy and ALL of them were mean so I think she won, hers were worse than mine. When we worked Inez's cattle we always had a bale feeder in the middle of the lot, so we had something to get behind when necessary.

The last bunch of really crazy calves I had, before I quit using a Simmental bull, by the time Doc Kinkead and Bryan McHugh finished working them we had two pickups and a tractor rammed against the pen fence, and we really needed more. Every time 8 or 10 of those crazy bastards hit the fence we would hear another wood post snap off. When we finally got done there weren't very many good posts left.

By the time I got most of the crazy bred out of my cattle, every gate around the lots and loading pen had the top pipe bent down, where a cow or big calf had been on top of it. And some of those crazy-assed calves could clear a gate flat-footed, without even touching it.

It sure is nice to finally have cattle I can walk through without risking a serious stomping.

*   *   *   *   *

Bud Johnson and Richard Head used to own some roping horses. When I was running my wild crazy cattle they bought a draft of my steers one Wednesday at the Sale Barn, to train their horses with. The next Wednesday the steers were back at the Sale Barn, Bud said you couldn't rope a calf if the horse couldn't catch it.

Cliff Kennett bought some of my crazy calves one year. He intended to bucket feed them, but every time they saw him with a bucket they started bouncing off fences. It was three weeks before Cliff took the calves back to the Sale Barn, it took him that long to get them in the loading pen.

*   *   *   *   *

Doc Kinkead

One fall I was helping Inez work her crazy old Simmental calves. James Earl Grant would catch them in the headgate, Doc Kinkead would give them some shots, then squat down behind the bulls and cut them, while I tailed them for him.

Doc squatted down behind one big old calf and cut the end off its sack. Pretty soon he said, "Well, I never in my life saw anything like that before, there's nothing in his sack but fatty tissue." Inez stood there with her hands on her hips, then said, "Well Doc, you silly old thing, you cut that calf last spring!"

*   *   *   *   *

Back in the early 1980's Doc Kinkead was at the farm one afternoon, working my cattle. I had several young cows, several really old cows, and a bunch that I wasn't quite sure about, so Doc was aging the ones I wasn't sure of.

We ran one cow into the chute that I knew had been around for several years, and after Doc checked her teeth I asked, "Is she a keeper, Doc?" He replied, "Oh hell yes, she's short-solid, a veritable heifer in your herd!"

Damn smart-assed vets, anyhow.

* * * * *

There are quite a few Doc Kinkead stories floating around out there, and I 'spect most of them are true, but if you ever have an old hound dog that gets shot all to hell by some no-good chicken-shit deer hunter, Kinkead is a pretty good person to have around. He sure 'nuff saved old Leon, and he worked pretty cheap while he was doing it, too. THANKS, DOC!

* * * * *

J.R. Jacobs always had really nice Shorthorn cattle. One spring he bought a young bull from Fred Coats. Marlon Landhuis saw J.R.'s bull, and decided he needed a bull like that to put on his cows. Marlon went to Fred's a couple of weeks later and picked out a bull. When Fred priced the bull Marlon had a fit. He told Fred "That's exactly the same price you charged J.R. Jacobs for his bull, and he's got twice as many cows as I do!"

The sad part is, Marlon actually thought that remark made sense.

* * * * *

David Fenton told me that when he used to make farm calls with Doc Kinkead that he thought Bill Blackwell, James Earl Grant and me were about the oldest people he'd ever met. Hell, we weren't much over 40 years old at that time. David said, "You know, I'm older now than you all were back then." Sure 'nuff, David, a lot older.

*   *   *   *   *

Marcia didn't mind fussing at me a little bit if she thought I needed it, but she was pretty protective if someone else started fussing at me.

When I rented the Cavcey Place the northwest corner of the farm backed up to Juniper Ridge subdivision, with just a woven wire fence between the farm and some duplexes. Usually when new tenants moved in, they thought they had a good disposal area for yard waste, beer cans, and other miscellaneous trash. This little corner of the farm was only accessible on foot, and whenever I was walking the fence and discovered trash I would throw it back over the fence, as far into the yards as I could. This didn't make for real friendly relationships with the neighbors.

Marcia answered the phone one day when I wasn't home, and a man asked to speak to me. She told him I wasn't there and offered to take a message. He told her his name and where he lived, then snapped "I want to know what he intends to do with this dead cow?" When Marcia asked him what dead cow, he replied "The dead cow across the fence from my house. It stinks, and I want to know what he intends to do with it!"

My Baby apparently didn't like his attitude. She said, "Well, if the cow is dead he doesn't need it, you can have it if you want it," and then she hung up on him. A few minutes later he called back and apologized, so she told him she was sure I didn't know the cow was there, and that I would take care of it.

It was at least 250' from the cow to the nearest spot accessible with a tractor, and I used all of the chain, cable and heavy rope that I had, getting hooked onto the cow. She was starting to get kind of soft, and I was a little worried that she might come apart when I drug her across the ditch, but except for a few gobs of hair and some juicy ooze she made it across in one piece. I still laugh whenever I think about what must have run through that guy's mind when Marcia told him he could have that dead cow.

*   *   *   *   *

There are always a few things that stick in your mind that you wish you had a picture of. When Justin and Clint were 5 or 6 years old, Bryan McHugh came out to Mom's farm to do a post mortem on a cow that had died for no apparent reason. I had drug her into the edge of the woods with a tractor, and she was laying on her back, spraddle-legged.

The boys watched intently while Bryan split her open and worked his way through the guts until she was eventually empty. I was talking to Bryan when I heard "Paw-Paw, look!" I turned around and saw the boys standing waist deep in the gutted cow, one of them holding the lungs over his head, and the other one holding a bloody liver. They were grinning from ear to ear. Bryan and I almost cracked up, I'd give anything for a picture of that. The only bad part was, those two little blood soaked varmints had to ride home in the cab of my truck.

*   *   *   *   *

When I was a kid Pappy and Grandpap never left their bull with the cows year around. He would be sorted off in the fall, and he spent the winter on the opposite side of the road, usually with one old Grandma cow to keep him company. Around the middle of June he would be turned in with the rest of the cows. One year when I was 6 or 7 years old we were walking the bull back across the road. He knew where he was going, and he started bellering as soon as he headed towards the road. The cows heard him, and when he got to the gate they were waiting for him. We let him in, he sniffed 4 or 5 cows, and when he found one that suited him he bred her immediately. When he was finished Grandpap looked at Pappy and said, "William, I believe he did her some good, she's got a hump in her back."

I thought about that remark for just a moment, then asked "Grandpap, did you ever put a hump in Grandma's back?" WHOP! WHOP! Grandpap smacked me and my little ass smacked the ground. That's the only time I can remember Grandpap ever smacking me, but it sure 'nuff got my attention, 'cause I guaran-damn-tee that was the last time I ever asked Grandpap any questions about hump-backed women.

*   *   *   *   *

In the book *A Full Cup of Joe* by Joe G. Dillard, Mr. Dillard talks about the "fa-woosh" sound that is made when the burner fires on a hot-air balloon. That sound is the bane of all cattlemen. Cattle will stand and nervously watch a damn balloon until the burner fires, then they run. If there's a fence in front of them they run through it, causing un-told hours of bull-shit, trying to get spooked cattle back home. If there's a ditch or creek in front of them they run into it, risking broken legs or other injuries.

When Pappy was in his late 70's, a balloon had run some of our cattle through a fence twice in one month. He called Charlie Foster, who was Boone Co. sheriff at the time, and told Charlie that if he knew who was flying that balloon he needed to tell them that if they flew low over Pappy's farm again they would be shot down. Charlie said, "Now Mr. Easley, you don't really mean that." Pappy said, "Oh yes I do, Charlie, I really mean it!"

I don't know if Charlie contacted the balloon pilot or not, but the balloon didn't come back, and it's probably a good thing it didn't because there's no doubt in my mind that Pappy would have taken a shot at it. He didn't get mad very often, but when he got mad he did whatever he thought was necessary to solve the problem.

*   *   *   *   *

I hate hot-air balloons, I flat-ass hate them! I guess if the only livestock you owned was a parakeet and a house cat balloons would be fun to watch, but when you have cattle they're just a damn pain in the ass.

Several years ago stray dogs were giving James Earl Grant and me fits one fall. We couldn't ever get close enough when it was happening to eliminate the problem so the dogs kept chasing our calves. Mine had gone through the fence once and scattered all over the neighborhood, and bounced off the lot fence so many times there wasn't much fence left. James Earl's calves had been out a couple of times, getting as far north as I-70 one morning a couple of hours before daylight. That episode wasn't much fun.

One afternoon I was out by my machine shed when I spotted a balloon floating in from the west. It was gradually getting lower as it came my way. After passing over without firing that damn noisy burner it headed in the direction of Grant's. A car stopped in the road and a young lady got out and was watching the balloon as she talked on a handheld CB radio. I walked out to the road and asked her if she was in contact with the balloon pilot. She smiled and assured me that she was. I pointed my finger in her face and said "Young lady, I want to tell you something. That balloon is headed right towards James Earl Grant's cattle lot. Dogs have been chasing his cattle and they're pretty spooky, so if you can talk to that guy you'd better tell him not to fire that burner when he's anywhere close to that pen of cattle because if he does I'll guaran-damn-tee those calves will go through the fence."

So far she hadn't seemed very concerned, but I finally got her attention. I said, "And I'm gonna tell you one more thing. If he runs those calves through the fence, there are gonna be a bunch of people out here who get in their vehicles and start following that balloon, and there will be at least one of them there when that thing lands, and it ain't gonna be pretty!" By the time I finished talking she was jabbering on her radio, then she jumped in her car and headed east with gravel flying. I got in my truck and drove over to Grant's in time to watch the balloon float silently over James Earl's pens, with the calves looking up watching it. The guy was getting pretty low but he floated over Grant's house without firing the burner, and was a reasonable distance on the other side of the road before he finally got so low that he had to fire it, but by then he was far enough away from the calves that it didn't spook them.

I don't know what that girl told the pilot, but it sure 'nuff got his attention, and it's a good thing that it did, because we were all sick of chasing calves, and if he'd run them through the fence I'll guaran-damn-tee that when he landed it wouldn't have been pretty!

*   *   *   *   *

When I rented the Murphy Farm my bull and Gene Brown's bull had a disagreement one afternoon and took out at least 30' of good fence before they settled their differences. It was a lot easier to get to the fence from Gene's side, so the next morning we loaded posts, wire and tools into Gene's truck, and headed for the wrecked fence. Devin was 4 or 5 years old, and he came along to help us.

It took about an hour of driving posts and splicing and stretching barbwire, but we finally got the fence back in pretty decent shape. We sat down on the tailgate and Gene pulled out a pack of Red-Man and took a big chew. Gene offered some to Devin, but he just shook his head and made a face. I pulled out a can of Skoal mint and said, "Try this Devin, it's a lot better than that nasty old stuff your daddy chews." Devin quickly said OK, and stuck his thumb and two fingers all the way to the bottom of the can. He came out with all he could hold, shoved it to the back of his mouth, chewed about 3 times and swallowed. That probably wasn't a good idea. We loaded our supplies and headed back to the house with Devin in the middle. Before long I hollered "Brown, stop the damn truck!" He stopped and I pulled Devin out just in time for him to unload. We had to stop two more times before we got to the house. That was one sick little boy.

A week or so later I drove past Gene's house and he was in the front yard with Devin. We waved, and Gene told me that as soon as I passed, Devin said, "Dad, I like Alan, but he not give me no more tobacco, huh?" Gene replied, "No son, he not give you no more tobacco." Devin still remembers that little episode, and he told me that was the first and last time he ever chewed tobacco.

* * * * *

I'm sure everyone has heard of jumping mules. Well, I bought a roan Shorthorn bull from Duane Seicht one time that could put any jumping mule in the world to shame. That no-good bastard could stand flat footed and clear a 48" woven wire fence with 2 barbwires on top, and not even brush it.

One summer I had my cows and the old jumping bull on the Murphy Place. Eutsy Johnson informed me one afternoon that I couldn't turn a bull next to his property because he had registered cattle. I didn't have to turn my cattle into that field next to Eutsy's for a while, but I didn't like him telling me what to do, so before I left the Murphy Place that day I opened the gate and turned them in next to him.

In less than a week, old quickstep was over at Eutsy's, breeding registered cows. One morning I got James Earl Grant to help me go after him. We opened the fence between the fields and walked over to Eutsy's to drive the bull home. He was enjoying himself and he took offense at us trying to take him away from Eutsy's cows, so instead of us driving him back to Murphy's, he treed us behind a barbwire fence that circled a pond. I told James Earl to wait where he was and I'd go get my truck. I said, "I'll get behind him and I'll take him back to Murphy's or I'll run over him, but we're not going to walk around out here and let that son-of-a-bitch hurt us."

After I got in my truck I had to drive down the road about 1/4 of a mile and open a couple of gates to get into the field with the bull. When I pulled through the last gate I looked around, but I didn't see James Earl or my bull. I kept watching as I drove toward the pond, but I still didn't see anything. I thought "Oh hell, that crazy son-of-a-bitch has stomped Grant into that pond and drowned him." As I started to crawl through the pond fence to look for a body I heard James Earl holler. He was leaning up against a tree by Murphy's fence. When I drove up to where he was and asked him what happened to the bull, he told me the bull was over at Murphy's, where he belonged. When I asked him how in the hell he got the bull back in by himself, he said, "That son-of-a-bitch kept coming up to the fence bellering and pawing the ground, and the last time he did it I picked up a flint rock about the size of my fist and hit him right between the eyes with it. He jumped about 4' right straight up, bellered and headed for Murphy's at a dead run."

Eutsy got some nice gray-roan calves out of the deal. When Doc Kinkead worked the calves the next year, Eutsy said "I don't know where those calves came from, there wasn't a bull anywhere around when those cows got bred."

James Earl Grant, Cloe, and me, talking about things that sure 'nuff happened.
Cattleman's Advocate Photo by Susan Denkler, used with permission.

*   *   *   *   *

Edwin and Kitty Gordon lived across Range Line Road from Grants' for several years. Edwin always had some right decent black cattle.

One year he had been to a registered Angus sale and bought a couple of high-dollar yearling bulls. A few days later I was at Edwin's and he said there was something at the barn that he wanted me to see. When we got there the bulls were standing peacefully under a shade tree. Edwin asked me what I thought about his new bulls. I looked them over real good, then replied "I think you should have cut those common son-of-a-bitches before they got so damn big, they'd have been a hell of a lot easier to tail." That remark almost broke Edwin's heart, but he should have known I wasn't going to brag on his bulls and make him feel good.

*   *   *   *   *

When Greg and Jeff were 6 or 7 years old, Nanny (Marcia's mom) was at our house one afternoon when the boys got home from school. Before long she called out in a very worried tone of voice, "Marcia, look at the boys." They were out in the field east of the house with their pockets full of ear corn, and about a dozen cows were crowded around them so close you couldn't hardly see the boys. Marcia said, "Oh Mom, they're OK, they do that all the time. Those old cows are a bunch of pets, anyway." The boys were better off than Nanny was, she stood nervously looking out of the window, thinking of all the things that could happen to her little boys until they finally ran out of corn and returned to the house.

*   *   *   *   *

Marcia raised a big
garden for many years.
One summer she raised
way more cucumbers than
she knew what to do with,
so when some of them
would get really big and
start turning yellow she

would toss them over the fence. One young black white-
faced cow developed a taste for them, and when Marcia
was in the garden that cow would stand at the fence and
bawl until Marcia handed her a cucumber. My Baby
started calling that little cow "Cucumber" and the name
stuck. She was "Cucumber" 'til she finally went to the sale
barn 10 years later.

*   *   *   *   *

Pappy and Grandpap sold cattle at the Columbia
Livestock Auction from when I can first remember, and
from the 1970's until they closed I always sold my calves
there. It was a hell of a good auction barn at the time,
before Columbia pretty much crowded them out.

Bandy Jacobs, Logan Heathman, L.W. "Junior"
Angell, Luther and Charlie Angell, and when they got old
enough, Justin and Jon Angell pretty much kept things
moving. Until he had a stroke Junior Angell usually
started most of the cattle. He was getting up in years, but
he would set in the cage in the corner of the ring and price
cattle when they entered.

Cattle were cheap back then and it took a hell of a good
calf to bring 25 cents a pound. Junior was setting in the
cage one afternoon, starting cattle like he usually did. He
wasn't real interested in his work that day; he was dozing
off about half the time, and whenever some calves came

into the ring Junior would glance at them and usually say "20 cents a pound."

Once when a Hereford calf entered the ring Junior half opened one eye, glanced at it and said "20 cents a pound," just like he'd been doing. Bandy Jacobs said, "By God Junior, you better look at what you just did." Junior opened both eyes and took a better look. What he saw was a Hereford dwarf. It was well over a year old, but it had never seen 250 lbs. and probably never would. It was potbellied and its legs were just barely long enough to keep its belly from dragging the ground. It didn't have a switch on its tail, it had one white pop-eye and was almost blind in the other eye. It had horns about 8" long that grew straight out to the side, and it walked with its head held at a 90-degree angle so it could try to see a little something out of its best eye. It was a classic! Junior looked it over real good and said, "Hell, it's still worth 20 cents a pound."

Of course no one bid, so the calf went on out of the ring. About 30 minutes later it was back. Junior said, "12 cents a pound." No one bid, and the calf left the ring again. That sorry-assed calf came through the ring three more times that afternoon. The last time Junior started it for a penny a pound, but by then if he had offered someone $10.00 to take it no one would have done it, everyone was having too much fun laughing at Junior and his 20 cents a pound Hereford dwarf.

*   *   *   *   *

Years ago Herefords' were good cattle, and they're pretty much back to being good cattle again. However, for a really long time the dumb-assed show breeders did everything they could to ruin the breed completely. For some unknown reason they kept breeding them smaller and smaller until they damn near dwarfed them out of existence. Some Angus breeders did the same thing. There were some really sorry-assed black cattle around for a while, but like Herefords they've pretty much come back.

I've owned some good Hereford cows over the years, but all of the really good ones had brands on them and came from Colorado. For several years it was almost impossible to buy a decent Hereford cow that was raised anywhere close to home. It doesn't really matter how good the Herefords' and Angus get anyhow, I still like my Shorthorn cattle.

*   *   *   *   *

Bryan McHugh came out to the farm to work some calves for me in September 2013. He brought his portable chute and two good helpers, and Jeff came over to help. We were taking it slow and easy, vaccinating everything, tipping some horns and castrating 550 lb. bulls.

We had around a half dozen calves left, and everything had worked perfectly up to that point. I said, "You know, this is sort of like someone pitching a no-hitter through the seventh inning, everyone knows what's happening, but no one wants to jinx it by talking about it." Bryan nodded in agreement and no one said anything.

Bryan's son Matt was in the pen with me. I tapped a calf on the butt with my stick, he kicked, hit my stick with his foot and slapped the end of it into Matt's face. There wasn't any blood flowing, but we heard it smack when it hit him, and it had to hurt. As he stood there with both hands cupped over his mouth I remarked "Well Matt, damned old no-hitters are kind of over rated, anyhow."

*   *   *   *   *

I don't know exactly when cattle came to the old place on Bearfield Road for the first time, but I assume that when Grandpap's parents built their log cabin and moved to the farm in the early 1860's that they brought at least one old milk cow with them.

Grandpap raised cattle on the farm until he died in 1963, Pappy raised cattle there until he died in 1982, and I continued raising cattle on the old place until June 2014. Finally, surrounded by the City of Columbia on 3 1/2 sides, with Boys and Girls Town to the north, a City Park to the east, and a Catholic High School and a bunch of expensive houses to the south, I decided it was time to let them go. Getting out in the snow, rain and mud to feed cattle wasn't quite as much fun as it used to be anyhow, and since the old fences that I was patching on all of the time were the same old fences that I helped Pappy and Grandpap patch on when I was a kid, it just seemed like it was a good time to get out.

It's sort of the end of an era but there's just too damn much City of Columbia around the old farm anymore, and not nearly enough country.

The end of an era. Loading cattle from the old farm for the last time.

Bottle Babies

The best way to warm up a really cold calf is in the bathtub. Just carry that slick, dripping little rascal through the house and put him in the tub, but unless you've got a hell of a good water heater you'll be out of hot water by the time the calf is warm. Towel him off a little, then turn your kids loose on him for a while with your wife's hairdryer. Do that, then get a bottle of colostrum down him, and if that doesn't bring him around he's probably past help.

After the bottle a calf will usually lay down and take a nap. When you finally hear those little hooves clicking on the tile or hardwood floor, you know it's about time to take him back to his Momma. Quick, before you get stuck with another damn bottle calf.

*   *   *   *   *

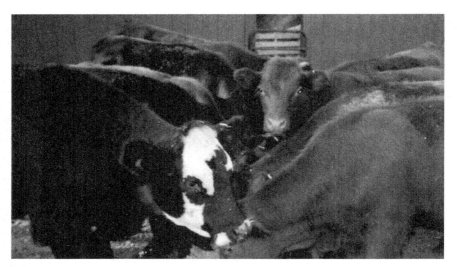

Pet yearlings

"I wanna be a pet yearling when I grow up!"

I've owned my share of wild cattle, but we've also had lots of pet cattle over the years. The 1st one I can remember was an orphan calf named "Curly" that I took care of when I was 6 or 8 years old, from bottle baby to 1200 lbs. When Curly was ready to butcher I said, "Oh no, we can't eat my Curly," so I was told that Curly was sold and a replacement steer was bought and butchered. When I got a little older I wondered about that a few times, but I never asked.

*   *   *   *   *

I listened to the Grand Old Opry a lot when I was a kid, so a couple of steers that I raised one year were named "Webb Pierce" and "Little Jimmy Dickens." I spent a lot of time that summer putting halters on those two stubborn rascals and then pulling on them 'til I ached, while they just stood there with their knees locked and looked at me.

Sis raised a couple of heifers named "Arabella Petunia" and "Arthoosia Mitilda." Pappy kept both of them for cows and they were around the place for a lot of years.

*   *   *   *   *

When Gene Otis worked for MFA in Columbia I used to sell him an orphan calf or the smallest twin occasionally. When I was crop farming I really didn't have time to fool with bottle calves, they're really just a big pain in the ass most of the time.

*   *   *   *   *

Old Tekotte called me one day and said "Bud, bring them damn boys up here, I've got something for 'em." What he had was two orphan lambs, a 25-lb. sack of milk replacer, and 2 brand new lamb bottles and nipples. Jay told the boys how to take care of their lambs and then we loaded them up and headed home. We rigged up a pen in the corner of the machine shed, and those lambs pretty much took over the place.

Every day when the boys would get home from school they'd let their lambs out, and it was a ball to watch them. Two or three times a week, Marcia would go out and set in a lawn chair and watch the show. The boys would chase the lambs, then the lambs would chase the boys, then the next thing you knew they would all be on the ground in a big pile. All of a sudden the lambs would jump up from the pile and make a mad dash over to Marcia so she could pet them on the head and tell them how pretty they were. They'd stand there for a moment, then they'd run back to the boys. They were probably the most entertaining critters we ever had on the farm.

When Jay sold his lambs, after they got them loaded into the trailer he told the buyer "I've got a couple of lambs on another farm, we've got to go get them." They buyer said no way in hell was he taking a couple of pet lambs. Jay told him to take them or unload the others, because they all went together. The boys were a little sad when they found out that their lambs were gone, but about 3 days later they got a check in the mail, and that made it seem a whole lot better.

May 1976. Jeff, Greg, and C.J. the beagle with Lambchop and Mutton.

*   *   *   *   *

On Easter morning 1978, I went to check the cows south of our house. As soon as I headed towards the creek I heard a cow bawl. When I got there, a 1st calf heifer was standing at the edge of the creek, and her new baby was in the creek, knee deep in mud, belly deep in water, and stuck. The heifer had tried to move him across the creek, but he had blundered off the crossing into the mud and water. I got him drug out, and then picked him up and slung him around my neck like a fur collar, and started slogging through the snow and mud towards the house, with water running down the back of my neck. The little heifer was walking along with us, so I detoured up to the barn and let her in, and then took the calf on to the house.

We soaked him in the bathtub 'til he was warm, then toweled him off a little and Greg and Jeff dried him good with Marcia's hair dryer. He had nursed before he got into the creek, so he wasn't really hungry, but we mixed up a bottle of milk and pancake syrup and he drank about half of it before he laid down on some bath towels and went to sleep. He spent a good part of Easter Sunday sleeping on those towels, but we finally heard his hooves clicking on the tile in the kitchen as he went exploring. Marcia and the boys played with him for a while, then I put a dog leash on him and headed for the barn, with the boys pushing him whenever he'd try to stop. The heifer saw us coming and she started bawling and was waiting at the gate to the barn when we got there. We opened the gate a little and pushed the calf through, and he immediately started nursing. By the next morning that calf didn't remember anything had happened to him, he was bucking around and running all over that stall. I never saw a 1st calf heifer as proud of her calf as that one was. When I let them out of the barn she immediately took her calf on a tour of the pasture, showing him off to all the other cows.

*   *   *   *   *

Several years ago in November I moved my cattle from the west side of Bearfield Road to the east side, for the winter. After we got them across the road and settled into their new pasture, we made a pass through the west side checking to see if we'd missed anything, but found nothing.

The next afternoon Fred Vom Saal called and said there was a real small black calf laying in the woods north of his house. Jeff and I went over and Fred told us where the calf was laying. She was pretty weak and

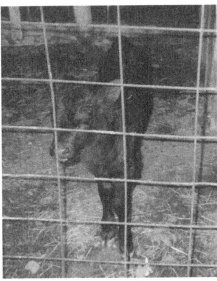

Miss Fred, November 2009

hungry, so she wasn't really much of a problem to catch. Jeff got in the back of the truck with her and we hauled her across the road and put her in the old hog shed. We fixed her a bottle of milk and pancake syrup, and as soon as she drank it she laid down and went to sleep.

Usually when a cow gets separated from her calf she'll bawl, walk the fence, maybe even jump the fence and go looking, but not this one. No bawling, no walking, nothing, I never even figured out which cow the calf belonged to. The only thing I could figure is that the calf was a twin, and as long as the cow had one calf she was satisfied.

We named the calf "Miss Fred" in honor of her savior, Fred Vom Saal. We decided pretty quick that a bottle calf in the winter, in a shed with no running water, wasn't going to be any fun, so we kept her for about a week to get her bottle-broke, then I took her to the sale barn. I hate to sell them that small, but sometimes they're just not worth the trouble.

Scenes from
Around the Farm

Brothers –
Uncle Edward and
Pappy in 1919 and 1966.

Outdoor Laundry, 1939. Mom, Pappy, and Grandpap.

Unloading Corn, 1950. Pappy and Grandpap in wagon, Mr. and Mrs. Brown on the ground.

Building our house, 1963

Me and some treasures that I found at the old place.

I cut as much wood as I ever did, it just takes a lot longer.

The Easley House
4500 S. Bearfield Rd.
Columbia, MO
1872-2015

Worthless Neighbors

Woodhaven Children's Home was Pappy and Mom's neighbor for several years. Sometimes they were fairly decent neighbors, but other times they were pretty sorry. At one point the staff that worked with the residents was pretty much overwhelmed. I don't know if they were under paid, under trained, under manned or what, but for a while the residents damn near ran the place.

John Brown worked on the Building and Grounds crew at Woodhaven for several years. One afternoon he was on a stepladder changing a light bulb when an attendant entered the room with a teenaged resident. The boy immediately rushed over to John and slammed into his ladder, tipping it over. John jumped and landed on his feet, unhurt. John said as the ladder hit the floor the boy looked at him and laughed, then said "You can't slap me, I'm retarded." The attendant apologized, then led the boy on out of the room.

John told mom that he hated to wish his life away, but he couldn't hardly wait 'til he was old enough to retire, so he could get away from that place. John didn't quite make it, he passed away from a heart attack while he was still employed at Woodhaven.

*   *   *   *   *

At some point after Marcia and I got married Pappy and Mom started locking their doors at night, but it never occurred to them to lock anything during the day.

About the same time as the incident with John Brown, an 8 or 9-year-old boy who lived at Woodhaven started coming over to Pappy's and Mom's house. He would rush in the back door, through their living room into the bathroom, then he'd shut the door and take a poop. Afterwards he'd stuff a whole roll of wadded up toilet tissue in the stool and flush it. Of course that would plug the stool and it would over flow all over the floor. Before cleaning up the mess Pappy and Mom would take the boy back to Woodhaven, and they were always told "We're sorry, we didn't know he was gone."

The last time they took him back, Pappy told whoever they talked to that he was getting tired of unplugging his stool. He said "If it happens again we won't bring him back, we'll call the Sheriff and report that someone broke into our house and is vandalizing it. When they get here we'll tell them where the boy lives, they can bring him back and you can work it out with the Sheriff's Department." Pappy and mom never saw the boy again, Woodhaven didn't want that kind of publicity.

*   *   *   *   *

During the same time period there was a severely retarded little girl who lived at Woodhaven. She was deaf and couldn't talk, but she loved water. Pappy found her in the creek 2 or 3 times, fully clothed, wading in waist deep water with a big smile on her face. When he would take her back he always received their stock answer, "We're sorry, we didn't know she was gone."

One morning that fall the temperature was just above freezing when Pappy went out to the barn. We had worked cattle a few days earlier and had forgotten to drain the stock tank after we turned them out. On the ground next to the tank Pappy found a pile of wet and muddy girl's clothes. He looked around and noticed the barn door was open, and when he looked in he saw the little girl curled up on the dirt floor, naked and nearly frozen. He put his coat on her and took her to the house. Mom found something for her to wear, and a very mad elderly couple stomped into the office at Woodhaven with one very cold little girl and a sack of wet clothes.

"We're sorry, we didn't know she was gone" just didn't cut it that day. By the time Pappy and mom got done talking they had made believers out of the people in that office, and the little girl never came back to the farm again.

*   *   *   *   *

Jim and Bruna Ortbals have been our neighbors east of town for many years. Bruna runs a 10 or 12 kid daycare center at their home.

During the time period when the residents were pretty much running Woodhaven, I used to find lots of soccer balls, footballs, colored rubber balls of all different sizes, frisbees, stuffed animals and other assorted toys on Pappy's farm. Some of them had floated down the creek and hung up in piles of drift and some of them had just been thrown over the fence.

For a while I would throw them back over the fence when I found them, but I finally decided if they were too damn lazy to come get them, I wasn't going to waste my time helping them out. I started tossing them in the corner of the barn and when I would collect enough to make it worthwhile, I would drop them off at Bruna's. For a couple of years I was unloading toys at Bruna's every 2 or 3 months.

Eventually Woodhaven changed administrators, the kids were supervised a lot better, and the toys quit floating down the creek. Bruna didn't get any more free toys, but I thought it was a big improvement.

$$* \quad * \quad * \quad * \quad *$$

At that time there was no city sewer line in the area, and Woodhaven had a right fair sized lagoon, located about 75' north of Pappy's property line, and maybe that far west of Clear Creek. One afternoon when Pappy went to check on his cattle, he found greenish-black water flowing down the creek. He followed it upstream and found some damned idiot who ran a septic tank service pumping the Woodhaven Lagoon into the creek.

It didn't take long for Pappy to get him stopped. He told the guy to get up to the Administration Office and tell them they were going to have some mad visitors very soon. Pappy went to the house and got Mom and then drove over to Woodhaven. When they walked into the Administrator's Office, his receptionist asked if she could help them. Pappy told her who he was and said he wanted to see Mr. Whatever. (If I ever knew the guy's name, I don't remember it now.) When the receptionist said she would see if he was available, Pappy said "I'll see for myself, young lady, thank you anyhow," and then he and Mom barged into the guy's office.

The shit-pumper had been there and warned him that some unhappy visitors were coming, and then he had left. That administrator planned to make short work of dealing with these two old country people. Pappy was trying to be nice, but everything he said the guy just waved it off. Finally he said "Oh, Mr. Easley, I don't know why you're so upset, it's no big deal." That remark caused Pappy to kind of come unglued. He said, "Mister, it's a big deal to me, and just for your information that creek runs through Rock Bridge Park, and it's probably going to be a big deal to them, to the Missouri Department of Natural Resources, and to the Missouri Attorney General's Office, and those are the three places I'm going to call as soon as I leave here."

In the length of time that it took Pappy to mention the Park, the DNR, and the Attorney General, that big-feeling old boy changed from an arrogant asshole into a groveling ass kisser. Mom said she thought that the guy would have given Pappy anything that he asked for. I thought Pappy was way too easy on them, but that's just the way he was. He settled for an apology, a solemn promise that it would never happen again, plus two months of weekly water testing, then two more years of random testing, by an independent lab.

The water in the creek never failed to test pure, but for the next 2 or 3 years whenever we'd cross the creek with a tractor or pickup, the water would boil up greenish-black behind the wheels. There's probably still some of that sludge settled into the gravel bars, but it's deep enough now that it doesn't show up anymore.

*   *   *   *   *

After Woodhaven revised their operations and farmed the residents out to off-campus group homes, Boys and Girls Town of Missouri purchased quite a bit of the old Woodhaven Campus. They were pretty rough around the edges for a while, but they improved over the years, and have actually turned into pretty decent neighbors.

Mom moved to a nursing home not too long after the transition, and Jeff moved into the old house. Boys and Girls Town has a "No smoking on grounds" policy, but most of their staff seems to smoke, so during break time there was always a group of people standing along the road smoking. Before long some of them started drifting south, and they would stand in front of Jeff's and toss their cigarette butts down in his yard. Some things piss Jeff off real quick, and that was one of them. He complained a couple of times, but it didn't seem to help.

Finally he picked up a bunch of butts and dropped them in a coffee can, then walked into the office at Boys and Girls Town, set the can of butts on the desk and told them he was sick of their damn cigarette butts in his yard. He suggested that they set a bucket of sand by their fence and tell everyone to put their butts in the bucket. Then he told them if that didn't work they really weren't going to like where he put the next coffee can full of butts that he picked up. I guess the message got across to them because that pretty much solved the cigarette problem.

*   *   *   *   *

Jeff was going to his mailbox one day when he saw a couple of 14 or 15-year-old boys in the field across the road, heading towards the old barn. He called to them to stop so he could talk to them, and they did. Jeff told the boys they were trespassing on private property, and he asked them what they were doing. One of the boys replied that they were just wandering around looking at stuff. One of them was carrying a long, heavy dog leash, and Jeff asked them what the leash was for, but they didn't really have a good answer for that.

When Jeff asked them where they lived they pointed in the general direction of Boys and Girls Town. While they were talking, Jeff called Kathi Vom Saal and told her to lock her doors because there were at least two boys from the home out prowling around, and there might be more. When Jeff asked the boys if the staff knew that they were wandering around, one of them said "Hell no, they had us locked in a bathroom, and we got tired of that shit so we kicked the window out and went for a walk," but they still couldn't explain where they got the dog leash, or what they intended to do with it.

Jeff told them it would probably be best if they'd let him take them back, but they said they didn't want to get locked in the crapper again. Jeff said if they didn't go back with him, he'd have to call the Sheriff and let him take them back. One of the boys said, "Oh man, don't call the Sheriff, he'll take us to the Juvenile Detention Center, and we don't like that damn place!" When Jeff told them those were their only two options, they agreed to let Jeff return them to Boys and Girls Town. They gave Jeff the leash, and followed him peacefully across the road. When he walked into the office with them the staff still hadn't missed them.

Kathi made a couple of phone calls to the right people that day, and things kind of changed after that. Even though they have turned into pretty decent neighbors, a home for handicapped children, or an almost teenage detention center is neither one really what you would choose to have adjoining your yard, but that's progress. Damn, ain't it great?

Damn Dumpers

The no-good pricks who dump trash on private property are not only too cheap to go to the landfill and pay a dumping fee, most of them are also too stupid to make sure that they're not dumping papers with their name, address, and maybe their phone number. If you can find this information in a pile of trash, the sheriff's department will damn sure make the sorry bastards come clean it up. I love it when that happens!

*   *   *   *   *

The first time I can remember a trash dumper getting caught is back when I was in high school. Someone threw a pretty fair sized truckload of stuff off the edge of the road south of our house, into the deep draw. Pappy poked around in the pile and found several magazines with a mailing address not over a couple of miles away. He called the Sheriff, and it seems an old widow woman had hired some MU students to clean out her garage. She had given them extra cash for the dump fee at the City Landfill, but they kept the money and tossed the trash out on Pappy's farm.

The old lady had thrown away the boy's phone number, so she called her son to clean up the mess. He was not happy about the situation. Pappy was at the trash pile with a Sheriff's Deputy while the clean-up was going on. Pappy was sitting on a big rock, watching, and the Deputy was leaning against his car as the guy climbed in and out of the deep draw time after time with buckets full of trash. With every bucketful he bitched a little louder. Finally the Deputy got tired of listening and said, "Sir, if you would have hauled your mother's trash to begin with, instead of making her hire someone to do it, we wouldn't have this problem, would we? You just keep carrying trash, and Mr. Easley will tell you when you're done."

*   *   *   *   *

When Greg and Jeff were little I hadn't switched to big round bales yet, so three or four times a week I would feed square bales at Pappy's. When I'd go down the road with the boys on the wagon, they'd always talk about the motorcycle in the deep ditch at the foot of the hill. I'd tell them it wasn't a motorcycle, it was just scrap-iron someone had thrown out. They'd say, "Oh no, Daddy, it's not scrap-iron, it's a motorcycle."

One day I stopped at the foot of the hill and slid off the edge of the road into the draw, so that I could tell them for sure there was not a motorcycle in the ditch. Damned if there wasn't a motorcycle in the ditch! All the good stuff was missing, it had been pretty well stripped but it was sure 'nuff a motorcycle. I was a lot tougher back then than I am now, so I drug that thing up out of the ditch, pushed it up onto the road and then loaded it onto the wagon.

When we finished feeding, I put it in my truck and took it to the Sheriff's Department. The serial number was still legible, and they quickly verified that it had been stolen about six months earlier. The deputy told me that if no one claimed it, after 90 days I could have it. Apparently someone claimed it and it's just as well, because that thing wasn't much of a prize.

*   *   *   *   *

When I rented the coal mine farm north of Columbia that is now the city landfill, I started to pull into the field one day to check my beans but I couldn't get off the road. Some worthless son-of-a-bitch had parked right in the gate and dumped a couch, an old recliner, a refrigerator carton half full of miscellaneous trash, and several grocery bags full of magazines and papers. I dug through it, and the only thing I could find with a name on it was a couple of boxes of wedding invitations from the early 1960's. I wish I had saved one so I could tell you who the people involved were, but I didn't. Anyhow, Mr. and Mrs. _____ and Mr. and Mrs. _____, of Columbia, MO, were inviting people to their kid's wedding.

At that time, the Sheriff's Office was still in the Courthouse downtown, so I drove to the office and went in. When a Deputy asked if he could help me, I tossed a wedding invitation on the counter, and told him where I found it. He read it, then asked me if I would like to have the trash cleaned up if he could locate the people. I said, "I'd rather see you hang the sorry bastards off the courthouse columns, but if you can't do that, I'd settle for getting the trash removed."

He stood there for a moment, then said, "I'd have to do some checking, but I don't think that I can hang them for dumping trash, but if they're still around Columbia, I guarantee they will clean it up for you." I'll say one thing, that deputy was on the ball. I went by the field just before dark, and not only was all of the trash gone, there were broom marks in the dirt. He had definitely made believers out of them. I just wish I had gotten there in time to watch them clean up their mess, but it's probably best that I didn't.

*　　*　　*　　*　　*

When I farmed Shirley Abbott's place at the SW corner of Rangeline and New Haven Roads, I started to pull in the field one day and there was a big pile of ashes, burned tin cans and broken glass in the gate. Some sorry bastard had backed in and dumped his trash-burning barrel. He'd also dumped some cardboard boxes, sheetrock scraps and a FOR SALE sign with a phone number hand written on it.

Larry McCray was a deputy sheriff at the time, so I called him and told him the phone number. A couple of hours later, Larry called me and said the trash should have already been cleaned up, and he asked me to check and see. When I called him back I said they'd done pretty good, except for some ashes and a few glass shards. Larry said, "Pretty good doesn't cut it." I don't know what he told them, but the next time I checked that gate, it looked like the living room floor.

That's not the only time Larry got something done for me. I really miss having someone at the Sheriff's Department that I actually know. It made a hell of a difference.

*   *   *   *   *

Several years ago, some asshole started leaving plastic bags of yard waste, oil cans, used oil filters, and plastic jugs of old oil, in the middle of the lane that goes to Mom's barn.

I hand painted a sign, "No Dumping, you SOB." and nailed it to a tree near the road. It worked for over six months. Finally one day when I pulled off the road, the sign was in the middle of the lane, with trash piled on top of it. Oh, well.

Magic Fingers and Clean Spots

Justin started following me around as soon as he was able to walk. When he started going to the field with me he was so little that I would take a stack of diapers along. If we went to James Earl's Parlor, Modern Farm Equipment Co, MFA or Bourn Feed, as soon as we'd get out of the truck I'd hold out my hand and say, "Grab my magic finger." He would grab my little finger and follow me wherever I went. One day he asked me why my finger was magic, and I told him because as long as he held onto it he could go everywhere I went.

One day we were walking across the parking lot at James Earl's, when Linda Hickam remarked that she couldn't tell who was leading who. After Clint came along, I usually had a kid on each hand. By the time all of those boys were old enough to follow on their own, my magic fingers were just about worn down to a couple of nubs.

*   *   *   *   *

When Greg and Kadi lived in the trailer back of our machine shed, I took Justin home one afternoon, after one of our tours. As soon as he walked in, he told Kadi he was hungry. She told him to go wash his hands and she would fix him a sandwich. He rubbed his hands on his pants real hard and said, "I'll just wipe 'em on my britches. That's what we wear 'em for." Kadi looked at me and said, "I wonder where he learned that?"

When any or all of the boys were with me and one of them would drop some food, I would pick it up and blow the dust off of it and say, "It's okay, it fell on a clean spot." One day, Clint dropped a cookie on the floor at Greg and Kadi's, so Kadi said she would get him another one. He picked it up and blew on it, then said, "It's okay, Mom, it fell on a clean spot." Kadi just looked at me and shook her head.

The floor in James Earl's Parlor wasn't exactly clean. There were 2 or 3 spit cans setting around, but people didn't always hit them. Add some cow manure, spilled beer, and maybe some dog piss, and it just wasn't very sanitary. One afternoon, Justin dropped a cookie in the Parlor. He picked it up and blew on it, then said, "It's okay, it fell on a clean spot." James Earl jumped out of his chair and grabbed that cookie out of Justin's hand, then said, "Oh hell no, don't eat that cookie, Justin, there aren't any clean spots on this floor!"

Neighborhood Stories

I've known Dan Cornell for a long time. I was farming the Ruggles Place North of I-70 when he and Barb got married, and they rented one side of the big house for a while. If I don't run into Dan anywhere else, I'll usually see him 2 or 3 times a year at his Pharmacy.

Several years ago I attended a neighborhood consignment auction that Bandy Jacobs was conducting in the parking lot at the Pierpont store. The auction had already started when Dan arrived, and he walked up just as Bandy was starting on a big pile of tools. When Bandy picked up an old Stillson pipe wrench Dan remarked to me that he would like to have it to hang on the wall of his shop. That was before the old Stillsons' became collectable, so he got it for a couple of bucks. Bandy asked, "What's your number, Cornell?" When Dan said he didn't have one, Bandy replied "Gotta have a number, go get you a number." After Dan left, Bandy picked up 2 or 3 more Stillsons'. I bought them, and when Bandy asked for my number I told him they went on Cornell's number. Bandy grinned, then held up some more Stillsons' and asked "Easley, do you think Cornell needs these?" I replied, "Why hell yes, and more if you've got 'em."

When Dan finally got back with his number Bandy grinned and said "Cornell, that's your pile of Stillsons, you need to take care of them, Easley and I don't have time to look after your stuff for you." Dan looked at that pile of wrenches, then he looked at Bandy and me and just stood there shaking his head.

I was nice about it though, I helped Dan carry the wrenches to his truck. It took us two trips a piece to get 'em all. For years after that, if Bandy picked up an old Stillson at a sale he would look at me and ask "Easley, where's Cornell?"

*   *   *   *   *

Once after Ed Riley had sold a load of hogs, someone on the job asked him if he had made any money on them. Ed replied, "I didn't really make any, just kind of bunched it up." It seems like that happens a lot when you try to farm for a living.

*   *   *   *   *

Bob Riesenmy worked for me off and on for several years before our boys got big enough to help. Except for Kevin Brown and Randy Blackwell he's probably the only person who ever worked for me who didn't tear up a bunch of stuff. He didn't know anything about farming when he started, but he was willing to learn and he was always careful with my equipment. Bob cut a bunch of saw logs on LeRoy Sapp's place one year, and he used my tractor to drag them out of the woods and load them. He traded me enough fencing planks to build the lot and loading pen at my barn. Bob and Maggie run a Country Store at Wilton, and I still see them occasionally.

*   *   *   *   *

Tommy Stewart left the gate open and his mules got out so many times that his renters finally posted a sign,

"TOM, SHUT THE GATE." Now if we can just get him to read the sign!

Tommy and Gene Brown must have gotten their gate training at the same place. Gene is so famous for leaving gates open that he made Lewis Baumgartner's column in "The Missouri Ruralist."

*   *   *   *   *

Milt Miller was on the New Haven School Board for a while. He lived in the El Chaparral subdivision, and was a teacher, professor, or something of the sort at MU, and he was definitely proud of the fact.

When Jim Myers sold his farm to Emory Sapp and Sons for the subdivision, he kept 10 acres with the house, old barn, and his collection of worn out machinery, AKA "damn junk." One night at a school board meeting Milt was whining about Jim's barn and junk collection. He said, "There ought to be some way the county could make that old man clean up that mess and get rid of that ugly old barn." I asked him, "Milt, when you were getting ready to buy your house did you drive out at night to look at it?" When he said no, I replied, "Well, Milt, if you came out in daylight you should have been able to see the barn, and if it offended you, you should have bought a house somewhere else. The barn was there before that damn subdivision, and anyone that doesn't like it ought to move."

Pissed him off! Oh, well, it pisses me off when people move out from town and want to change the country.

*   *   *   *   *

When I first rented Oscar Elley's farm across Rangeline Road from Tekotte's, Oscar was well up in his 80's, but he could still get around pretty good. He had a

1955 Chevy truck with a 16' bed built out of 2" rough sawed oak lumber, with 12" sides and no tailgate. Oscar had used the truck when he moved houses for a living. I don't know why he didn't ever get a ticket, the old truck probably weighed 7500 lbs. empty, but Oscar ran 6000 lb. plates because they were so much cheaper.

The first afternoon that I started combining Oscar brought the truck to the field and told me he wasn't busy, so he was going to help haul beans. He had a couple of 2x4's wedged slonch-wise in the bed near the back, supposedly to keep beans from running out. I dumped 40 or 50 bu. of beans on the truck, and that was all that was going to stay on. Oscar hauled that load and another one like it, and that was the last I saw of him 'til I was done cutting beans.

I had the farm rented on a crop share basis, and Oscar was supposed to pay me for half of the combining and hauling. When I went by to settle up, Oscar said that since he hauled part of the beans and I hauled part of them, we might just as well call the hauling even. Oscar was a little hard of hearing, and he could be plumb deaf when he wanted to be, so I didn't even try to argue the point, it wouldn't have done any good.

The next spring, I bought the old truck from Oscar. I did some work on the bed and used it for several years, until the engine blew up one day when I was driving on I-70, near Lake of the Woods.

*   *   *   *   *

I don't recall ever hearing Jack Glenn say a cuss word. He told me once that he wasn't offended by other people cussing, but it was just something he chose not to do. Jack's oldest son, Frank, might cuss a little bit from time to time, but his youngest son, John, knows all the words and uses them at every possible occasion. The only exception was when Jack was around, John never cussed in front of his dad.

It didn't really matter where John and I ran into each other, his standard greeting was always "Hi you damned old sow-bellied slut!" I pulled in at Glendale Farms one afternoon and Jack, Frank, and John were standing in front of their barn. After I got out of my truck, Jack and Frank greeted me, then John said, "Hello Mr. Easley, how are you today?" I looked at him and said "Mr. Easley? What's this Mr. Easley crap, why don't you call me a damned old sow-bellied slut, like you usually do?" John was so embarrassed he almost peed his pants, and Jack and Frank almost busted a gut trying not to laugh out loud. I enjoyed every minute of it.

*   *   *   *   *

R.J. Estes didn't believe in pissing away a bunch of money buying truck licenses. He had 3 old grain trucks, and he always bought a license for one of them. He had a couple of hooks made out of #9 wire, and whichever truck he used, he hooked the license plate onto the front bumper.

The Highway Patrol doesn't cut farmers near as much slack as they used to, I don't 'spect R.J. could get by with that today.

*   *   *   *   *

When I first started doing business with Russell Coats at Como Tire Supply, the store was located in the old building east of Columbia Welding, where Lee's Tire is located now.

One afternoon David Vaught was trying to mount a very stubborn combine tire for me. He'd aired it up halfway and broken it back down 2 or 3 times, and it just wouldn't pop out. He had brushed it good with soap and was starting to air it up again, when I took the lid off the bottle and poured the gap around the rim completely full of liquid soap. I stepped back, and Russell walked up just as that tire popped out. It drenched Russell with soap from the knees up. His face turned red and he spun towards David and was just ready to start chewing ass when he saw me standing there with the soap bottle in my hand. I grinned and said "Hello, Coatsy," then I looked at David and said "Hell, David, that's how you soap a damn tire so it'll pop out!"

Russell stood there just a moment with his teeth clinched, then he turned and walked back into the office. David said, "I sure am glad you were holding that soap bottle, because I was fixing to get one hell of an ass-chewing." I don't know if Russell remembers that little incident or not but David says something about it every once in a while.

*   *   *   *   *

Larry McCray was the 1st one in our neighborhood to own a 4WD truck. It was a late 1960's Ford. Larry named his truck "Geraldine." Geraldine was the sickest color green of any truck I ever saw, but she sure could take a lot of abuse.

If I got up on a Sunday morning and looked out at 4" or 5" of snow, with a good wind piling up the drifts, I could safely assume that before very long I would hear Larry on the CB radio, "Plow Boy, get your coat on, Pig Pokes' headed your way at a high rate of speed." James Earl Grant, Bill Blackwell, or Zane Dodge might already be in the truck and we would go drift-busting, just to see how far we could get before we got stuck.

Larry McCray, early 1960's, when we were both still pretty much kids.

Larry would have shovels in the back, and when we got stuck we would dig our way out, and maybe even put on a set of chains in the middle of a drift. If it got really bad, we might end up with chains on all four wheels before we got back to the house. Looking back, that seems like it was a hell of a lot of work, and freezing our asses off for nothing, but we sure had a lot of fun at the time. And it's just possible, that maybe there was a pint of Peach Brandy or Peppermint Schnapps under the seat of Geraldine, just in case our asses got really, really cold.

*   *   *   *   *

I cut wheat for Eutsy Johnson a couple of times, north of where Old Hawthorne Golf Course is now located. The whole project was pretty much a pain in the ass.

The bridge on Eutsy Lane had a 5000-lb. load limit and was way too narrow to cross with my combine. I had to go north to Richland Road, come in Cecil Zumwalt's driveway, through his barn lot, then drive across his farm and take down the fence between Cecil's and Eutsy's. Then when I did get started cutting, 250 bu. was about all it was safe to haul across that shackle-dee-assed bridge. In between the bridge and the field were 5 gates. The 1st year that I cut for Eutsy, Bob Riesenmy hauled for me, and I didn't realize quite how much of a hassle it was getting in and out. The next year when I used my truck, I opened and shut 5 gates each time I left the field with 2/3 of a load, then I'd open and shut them again when I came back. I was never so sick of damn gates in all of my life.

At that time most people hauled grain for 8 cents or 10 cents per bushel. When I sent Eutsy his bill I charged him 15 cents per bushel. I figured that was a dime for hauling, and a penny a gate. He didn't like it a damn bit. He sent me a check for the combining, along with a hand-written note:

> Alan Easley —
>
> I got my corn hauled in January for 6 cents per bushel!
>
> Eutsy Johnson

I sent him a note back:

> Eutsy Johnson —
>
> You got your wheat hauled in July for 15 cents per bushel!
>
> Alan Easley

He paid me, but needless to say I didn't have to open any damn gates on his place the next year, which was fine with me. I was sick of his rocks, gates, attitude and that damn shackle-dee-assed bridge.

*   *   *   *   *

When Devin Brown turned 16, Gene bought him a little 2 WD Ford Bronco. Devin thought since it looked like a 4WD vehicle he could go anywhere he wanted to go in it.

One night the temperature was around 20 degrees, there was 3" or 4" of snow on the ground and it was still snowing. Our phone rang around 10:30, and it was Devin. He asked, "Alan, where are your tractors?" I told him one of them was in the shed and the other one was setting out in the snow, wishing it was in the shed. He said, "Would you bring one of them up to Mom's and pull me out, I'm kind of stuck?" I said, "Hell, no! I'm not about to try and get a tractor started tonight and drive up there in this weather." I told him I would come up in my truck and see if I could pull him with it.

He was damn sure "kind of stuck." He had run up the back side of a pond dam, but didn't get turned soon enough to miss the water. I told him to hook onto something solid, because I was going to take a running start. I slammed him pretty hard a couple of times, and finally got his dumb ass drug to the top of the hill. I suggested to him that he might want to park that Bronco and go to bed, because that was what I was going to do, and I didn't intend to get up and make a second trip.

*   *   *   *   *

The next spring our phone rang one night around 9:00. Devin said, "Alan, my Bronco's stuck. I'm calling from Casey's (the "C" store on Rt. WW), could you pick me up and pull me out?" That was just what I'd been wanting to do, so I got in my truck and headed for Casey's.

When I got there Devin walked out, and he was soaked from the hips down. I asked him what happened and he said he was stuck over by Highway 63, and he had cut through the woods and waded the creek to get to Casey's. Devin looked like he was about frozen, so when he got in the truck I told him I had too many clothes on, then I turned the heater off and rolled the window down. He didn't appreciate it, but there wasn't much he could do about it.

At that time Stadium Blvd. quit at Highway 63, and there was just a narrow gravel track that led north to the water tower. Near the tower was a little hay field, and Devin had been out in the field making ruts. He'd gotten almost back to the road before bottoming out in a mud hole. The kid with him had been sitting in the Bronco with no heater running for well over an hour. He wasn't as cold as Devin, but he was getting pretty damned uncomfortable.

I pulled them out with no problem, and before I left I said "Devin, if you ever call me up at night to pull your ass out again, you'd better have a good-looking girl with you. If you pull out in the mud to get a little and you get stuck that's one thing, but riding around with some dumb assed boy and making ruts just for fun is something else. Don't call me again unless you've got a really good reason to be out in the mud."

I don't know if Devin quit acting stupid with his Bronco, or if he just started calling someone else, but I never had to pull him out again.

*   *   *   *   *

When Marlon Landhuis built his irrigation lake (that was never used for irrigation) he went to see Bill Blackwell and told him that the project engineer thought the lake would lay out a lot better if water could be backed onto Bill's farm at the upper end of the lake. Bill told Marlon to bring his brother, the engineer and the earth moving contractor out to the farm and explain exactly what they wanted to do, and then he would talk with them about their plans. Marlon said he would arrange a meeting.

A week or so later when Bill walked out of his house one morning to go to work he heard a dozer running. It sounded pretty close, so he got in his truck and drove to the backside of his place to see what was going on. The fence between Bill and Marlon had already been pushed out, one dozer was running on Bill's property and another one with a scraper was headed that way. Bill came unglued! That poor dozer operator got one hell of a cussing that morning. He kept trying to tell Bill that he was just doing what he had been told to do, but Bill wasn't really in a mood to listen. When he finally stopped to get his breath the operator told him that Marlon said he had talked to Bill, and he was in agreement with what they intended to do. Bill told him that Marlon was a lying piece of shit, and to get that damn equipment off of his property.

I don't know if Marlon paid for it or if the contractor got stuck with it, but Bill got a section of new fence and some grass seed where the ground had been disturbed. The engineers redesigned the lake and it was built without backing any water onto Bill's place. Marlon never mentioned the incident to Bill, it was just like it had never happened.

*   *   *   *   *

The day after Greg Michelson bought Marlon's farm, Marlon showed up at my place with a trailer load of gates. That was long after Marlon had been shot, and he was pretty much paralyzed and got around with a walker. He couldn't do anything himself, but he had some derelict with him who had apparently loaded the gates for him.

Marlon told me that when he sold the farm the gates didn't go with it, and he needed a place to store them until he bought another farm. I told him to pull over east of the house and lean them up against my big round bales. He said he'd rather put them where no one could see them from the road so I told him to pull around behind my machine shed. Something about this deal just didn't seem right, so I decided I wasn't going to get involved. Marlon's helper shoved the gates off the trailer and leaned them against the shed, then they left.

The day Greg Michelson bought the farm I had called him and told him I was interested in renting it. About a week after Marlon left the gates, Greg came over one morning to talk about a rental agreement. While we were visiting, Marlon's name was mentioned. Greg said "That man is something else. When I bought the farm there were a lot of good gates over there that were supposed to go with the place, but there's not a gate left and Marlon says he doesn't have any idea what happened to them." I smiled and said that I knew what had happened to them. I told Greg that Marlon had hidden them behind my machine shed, then I said, "I'll bet you'd like to have them back, wouldn't you?" Naturally he said yes, so I told him he was welcome to come get them anytime. I told Greg that when Marlon said he was looking for a place to store the gates where they couldn't be seen from the road that I figured Greg might be looking for them, so I told Marlon to go ahead and unload them here, where they would be handy to reload.

He came after the gates that afternoon, hauled them back to his place and leaned them against the fence west of his driveway. Greg said a couple of days later Marlon pulled in the driveway and when he got to the gate pile he slammed on the brakes and stopped, looked at the gates for a moment, then shoved his old truck into reverse and flew down the driveway backwards and shot onto WW without even slowing down or checking for traffic. He then headed towards town with his tires squalling.

Marlon never mentioned the gates to Greg or me again. Like most of Marlon's deals, it was just like it had never happened.

*   *   *   *   *

Years ago, when Bill Blackwell had his farm on Rangeline Road, and Marcia and I still owned the 80 acres east of our house that Jan Hayes owns now, I had the field north of Bill's in corn one year and Bill had a right decent size watermelon patch just across the fence from the corn field. When I was shelling corn that fall I climbed the fence 3 or 4 times and got a watermelon. I would reach across the fence and drop them, and they would bust up enough that I didn't even need to use my knife, I'd just pick up big chunks of ripe watermelon and eat them.

I saw Bill a few days later and he asked me if we were having any trouble with coons at our place. When I told him not really, he said the coons were raiding his watermelon patch. He said he didn't know for sure how they did it, but they were getting the melons clear over on my side of the fence before they ate them. I kinda grinned and said, "It's amazing what a hungry coon can do when he sets his mind to it, isn't it?" Bill grinned back at me and said "Yeah, isn't it?"

It was damn good watermelon and it sure beat going to the store and buying one!

*   *   *   *   *

When James Earl Grant and I first started farming Greg Michalson's place, neither of us had a corn-head for our combine, so we hired Don Copenhaver and Bill Streeter to shell our corn. They were farming together at the time, and were both employed at the MFA Home Office, but that was long before either one of them became President and CEO of MFA, Inc.

They would get off work around 4:00, then come to the field and shell corn 'til after midnight. Donnie would shell for a couple of hours, then he would rest while Billy shelled for a while. We were storing the corn in the bins on the farm, and James Earl and I took turns hauling from the combine to the bin. We were hauling with tractors and gravity-flow wagons, because it was a lot easier to unload wagons in the dark than trucks.

One night around 11:00 I had just finished unloading when an SUV pulled up to the bins, and a pretty young lady got out with a can of beer in her hand. Donnie was shelling at the time, so Billy walked over and said "Alan, this is Donnie's girlfriend, Jessi. Jessi, this is one of the guy's we're working for." I reached out and took the beer out of her hand and said, "Hello Jessi, I'm the Reverend Alan Easley, and I'd appreciate it if you didn't bring any more beer onto this farm!" I turned and threw her beer as far into the cornfield as I could throw it, then walked back to my tractor. As I was climbing on I heard her ask Billy if I was really a Preacher and he replied, "Yes he is, he farms during the week and preaches on Sundays." It was all I could do to keep from laughing out loud and ruining everything. They had a CB radio in the combine, and as soon as I got on the tractor and drove away, Jessi called Donnie and asked him the same question she had asked Billy. Donnie figured out real quick what had happened, and he replied, "He sure is, and I hope he didn't catch you drinking a beer!"

Donnie and Billy have both moved up the corporate ladder, and they're probably the only two CEO's that MFA has ever had who have shelled corn at midnight for a Preacher. David Grant still calls me "Reverend Easley" occasionally.

* * * * *

Most men call their wives by their name, or Hon, Babe, or some other form of endearment. Not old Tekotte. When talking about Ruth, Jay called her "Miz Hitler" or "The War Department." When he was talking to her he just called her whatever came into his mind at the time. Ruth was used to it, she'd just look at him and chuckle.

One morning I was standing in the kitchen at Tekotte's talking to Jay, when Ruth started out of the bedroom in her nightgown. Jay hollered "Run, Old Woman, we've got company." Ruth replied, "Oh, that boy's seen women in their gown tails before." Jay said, "By God, not any that are shaped like you. Run, woman, before you scare him to death."

* * * * *

Previously published in "Successful Farming," used with permission.

Back in the early 1970's, during the time before it was butchered up into 10 acre tracts and covered with houses, I rented Oscar Elley's farm across the road from Tekotte's.

One morning in November I was plowing right across from Tekotte's house. As I was turning at the far end of the field I lost the lynch pin from one of the lift arms, and the plow became partially unhooked. I usually carried some spares, but that morning I didn't have any with me. I cut some barbed wire off the fence and fastened the arm in position temporary, then headed across the field toward Tekotte's house to see if Jay had a pin I could borrow. He and Ruth were in the kitchen when I got there. I told him what I needed and he found several pins in a parts bin in his machine shed. When we got back to the house Jay said "Bud, you better come in and warm up a little while you're here, you've got all day to plow."

After Jay and I sat down at the kitchen table I asked Ruth if she was hoarding all of her coffee. She said that she didn't have any made, but that she supposed that she could make a potful if I wanted some. I told her that seemed like the neighborly thing to do, so she put on a pot, then we sat and visited while the coffee perked. That was before the era of automatic coffeemakers, so it was at least 20 minutes before the coffee was done perking. When it was ready Ruth got up and poured me a steaming cup of coffee. Just as she set the cup on the table in front of me, I jumped up and said, "Hell Ruth, I don't have time to sit here and drink coffee, I've got to go plow!" I grabbed my coat and was out the door before she could say a word.

I walked back across the road, installed the borrowed pin, and spent the rest of the day plowing. A couple of days later I met Jay in the road and we stopped to visit. Jay warned me "Bud, you better not come by the house for a few days unless you know I'm home, 'cause "Miz Hitler" is still pissed off at you, and if she kills you I need to be there, so I can tell Miss Marcia what happened." It took a few more days, but Ruth finally settled down. I don't know if she ever forgave me completely, but at least she got over her mad spell.

*   *   *   *   *

Previously published in "The Cattleman's Advocate," used with permission

Turner Farm Road has really changed since Marcia and I bought the farm and built our house in 1963. The old Parsonage at the corner of Olivet and Turner Farm Road was there, and across the road from where Jeff Bradley's house is now there was an old farm house that was rented out occasionally, then our house on the south side of the road, and katty-whompas across the road from us was "Dirty Elmer's" little shack. Back then from the little bridge east of our house (that Larry Cook later fell through with a lime truck) on east to Range Line Road, it was pretty much impassible for at least 6 months out of the year. When we heard a car coming we went to the door, because if they weren't coming to visit us they were lost, and were going to stop and ask directions.

There are now four Columbia school buses passing the house every day (two of the idiots drive like they were on I-70), there are weekly trips by the Central Dairy truck, a Swann's Ice Cream truck and two trash trucks, plus numerous cars and pickups speeding down the road at all hours of the day and night. It's still not exactly downtown (Thank God), but there are now 11 houses on the same 1 1/4 mile stretch of road, most of them on 3 acre to 10 acre tracts. Before Marcia died, she said that I needed to adapt to civilization but I told her that I was here first, and civilization needed to adapt to me.

One Sunday morning several years ago there was about 3" of snow on the ground, and the temperature was 10 degrees above zero. When I got up that morning, I rekindled the fires, drank some coffee, and then decided I'd read the morning paper before I went to the old home place to feed my cows. I knew that if I put on my long-Johns, insulated shirt and overalls, I would get way too hot while I was reading the paper. I didn't want to remove the overalls and shirt to put on the long-Johns when I got ready to leave, so I did what any normal person would have done, I put on the long-Johns only. Then my black knee length gum boots, a winter cap with the ear-flaps down, and to protect my hands a pair of heavy yellow chore gloves. Thus attired, I headed down the driveway to get the paper.

The snow did an excellent job of muffling the road noise, and I was bending over to pick up the paper before I realized that a car was coming down the road. I'm too old to run and there wasn't any place to hide, so I did the only logical thing. As the car passed, I stood there in my long-Johns, flashed my best smile, and waved. The two elderly ladies in the car damn near twisted their heads off as they turned around to look back at me as they passed. I don't know why they were out driving around on snowy roads on a Sunday morning because they definitely weren't from our neighborhood, and I don't have any idea where they were going but I'd almost bet that when they got there their first question was, "Who's that crazy old man who lives on the other side of the creek and wanders around in his underwear?"

I still go after the paper in my long-Johns, but I am making an effort to adapt to civilization. I now stop and listen real close before I get too far from the house.

CB Handles

Back in the 1970's and early '80's everyone in our neighborhood fell into the CB radio craze, like most other people at that time. It started out with some mobile units in our pick-ups with little short stick-on antennas', then most of us went to the tall, spring mounted stainless steel antennas' that country comedian Jerry Clowers called "a big old fishing pole on the back that goes whoosh, whoosh, whoosh when you stop." Then we put radios in our cars so our wives could talk to us, then most of us installed base units in our homes, so we could talk to each other at any time. Kind of like Facebook with no pictures.

Of course, everyone had a CB handle. Richard Rothermich was working at Boone Co. MFA at the time, and when MFA installed a base unit, Richard chose "Farmer's Friend" as their handle. One day when bean prices had dropped another dime, someone said, "With friends like that, I couldn't afford very damn many enemies."

Zane and Donna Dodge were "Loner" and "School Marm," Larry and Dolores McCray were "Pig Poke" and "Lady Poke," Bill and Doris Blackwell were "Blue Goose" and "Mother Goose," Gary and Lynn Chandler were "Silver Fox" and "Lady Fox," James Earl and Dorothy Grant were "Sneaky Snake" and "Bookworm," and Al and Charlene Brittian were "Dirt Digger" and "Snowflake." I was "Plow Boy" and thanks to Jay Tekotte, Marcia was "Pancake."

One cold Sunday morning I was helping Jay combine beans on Arno Winkler's farm, across the road from our house. Around 10:30 Greg and Jeff came to the field on their dirt bikes and told me breakfast was nearly ready. I told Jay "Old Man, I'll be back dreckly, I'm going to the house and eat some pancakes." The next time Jay saw Arno, he said, "I thought I'd heard that thing called about everything you could call it, but I never heard it called a pancake before." Of course, word of that got around to all of the neighbors, and Marcia took a lot of teasing about it. She said, "I ought to smack that old man, I really ought to smack him."

The day that Don Duffy installed the base unit in our house, it was a total damn set-up. As soon as that base was turned on, all the neighbors took turns calling for "Pancake, at that new Pancake base." Marcia hated that handle with a passion, but she never got mad about it, and it's just as well she didn't, because she was "Pancake" for as long as we had CB Radios.

The Boone County Fair

I had a lot of fun when I was on the Boone Co. Fair Board, but it's sort of like the School Board, it's a damn good way to piss people off. It doesn't matter what you do or how you do it, not everyone is satisfied.

One year when Hale and Helen Fletchall were Chairmen of the 4H calf show they were upset about something, as usual. Hale cornered James Earl Grant and me and started telling us how things were going to be done. The longer he talked the madder he got, and pretty soon he started shaking his finger in James Earl's face. That wasn't really a good idea. James Earl took it for a little while, then he reached out and clamped Hale's finger in his hand and bent it back just far enough that it started to get uncomfortable. Grant said, "Old man, if you want to talk I'll stand here and listen, but if you poke that damn finger in my face again I'll break it off and shove it up your ass!" He twitched the finger one more time, just to make sure that Hale understood him, and then turned it loose.

Hale dropped his hands to his sides and didn't raise them above his waist again until the discussion was over. I think he got the message.

*　　*　　*　　*　　*

The old Fairgrounds at West Boulevard and Worley was a far cry from the modern facility that we have now.

There was an old oak barn in the northwest corner of the Fairgrounds that wasn't good for anything except gate storage. Robert McGrath told me that the old barn was there when he was in Junior high school, of course at that time it was way out in the country. He said they would occasionally use the old barn as a rest stop when they walked home from school. Robert has a really interesting story involving the old barn. Ask him about it sometime when you see him.

*   *   *   *   *

Like most of the country kids, Jeff Wren started showing calves at the Fair when he was pretty young. One year Jeff had spent the night in the barn with his calves, and the next morning Bill Blackwell was talking to him, when Bill spotted Jeff's dad, Donnie, walking into the barn. In a loud voice Bill said, "Hey Whiskey Man, better hide those bottles, here comes your dad." Donnie thought it was pretty funny, but it almost embarrassed Jeff to death. Jeff's in his 40s now, but Bill still calls him "Whiskey Man" whenever he sees him.

*   *   *   *   *

Tater Fenton lived on West Boulevard, two or three blocks from the old Fairgrounds. Tater hated the Fair; he hated the noise, he hated the lights, he hated the extra traffic, and he damn sure hated the flies from the livestock barns.

One year during the Fair, Tater was at the Bull Pen raising hell about all of the flies. He said, "We can't even go out in our damn yard for the flies, those people ought to have to do something about all those goddamn flies on their cattle."

I said, "Hell, Tater, when those cattle come to town there is not a fly on them. Twenty-four hours later all of your damn kitchen flies are over there eating them up. You people that live near the Fairgrounds ought to have to do something about all of your damn flies." That was all it took to get Tater really cranked up. As soon as he got started good I paid Jackie Cockrell for my coffee and headed home, leaving Tater there for everyone else's listening pleasure.

*   *   *   *   *

The Fair was still located at the old Fairgrounds when I was serving on the Fair Board. Security was a lot more lax back then than it is now. Shortly after midnight the entry gates would be pulled shut, but not locked. There were always a few people sitting around visiting and drinking beer until 2 or 3 o'clock in the morning, but no one had a problem with that. The rowdy drunks were long gone, and anyone still there was just relaxing and enjoying life.

The first year that John Sam Williamson Jr. got back from the Air Force, he spent quite a bit of time at the Fair. One night another Board member and I (I think it was Clayton Grey, but it's been a long time, so??) were heading for our trucks around 2:00am. The FFA boys had a large round stock tank set up as a dunk tank, and as we neared the tank we spotted Johnny and a young lady soaking in the tank. For some reason Johnny really wasn't glad to see us.

As we got closer we could see most of their clothes folded and stacked neatly near the tank. We visited with them for a little while, then started tossing clothes into the tank. Johnny pleaded, cussed and threatened, but he wasn't really in any condition to get out of the tank so we just kept tossing clothes. Finally there wasn't anything left except a really fancy pair of brand new cowboy boots. When I picked them up Johnny said, "Oh no, Alan, not my new boots." I said, "Yeah Johnny, I think so." He told me his billfold was in one of them. I stuck my hand into one of the boots, and as I forced it underwater I said, "Damned if it's not, right there in the toe." There wasn't anything left to throw in the tank, and Johnny didn't seem like he wanted to visit with us anymore, so as his boots slowly sank to the bottom of the tank we told Johnny and his girlfriend to have a nice evening, then we walked on over to our trucks and went home.

We probably shouldn't have done that, but it sure seemed like fun at the time. SORRY, JOHNNY!

*   *   *   *   *

When I was growing up, Pappy and Grandpap never showed a ham at the Boone County Fair. Hams were cured to eat, and occasionally they would sell one to Tom Funk, but it never crossed their minds to take a ham to the Fair.

I always thought our hams tasted as good or better than anyone else's, and I was sure that they looked just as good, so in 1967 I told Marcia I was going to enter a ham in the Fair. We had butchered one hog the fall before, so I had 2 hams to choose from. The morning of the ham show I took the best one to the Fair on my way to work, and when I stopped on my way home to check on it I almost fell over when I found out it had won Grand Champion.

I showed hams off and on for 25 years after that. Some years my ham placed near the top, other years it didn't place quite so good, but it always made the sale. I eventually kind of lost interest, until our granddaughter

Leah joined the 4H ham project. She showed hams for two years and had the 4H Reserve Champion ham each year. When she got out of high school and joined the Marines that was the end of her ham shows.

Every ham that we entered in the Boone County Fair Ham show over the years was hickory smoked, but in 2013 the rules of the show were changed, and smoked hams were no longer eligible to enter. Where did they come up with that crap, what do those dumbasses think a Boone County ham is, anyhow?

$228 Paid for Champion At Fair's Ham Breakfast

August 6th, 1967. Pete Christus, left, and Sen. A. Basey Vanlandingham with Marcia and me and our Grand Champion ham at the 22nd annual Boone County Fair Ham Breakfast.
Columbia Missourian Photo, used with permission.

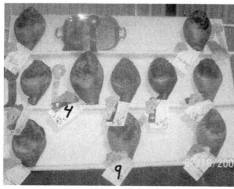

Boone County Fair Ham Show, 2009. Leah's Ham is #4, Greg's ham is #9.

Me and a Fair Ham, 2000

*   *   *   *   *

In 2012 The Boone County Fairgrounds suddenly became the "Central Missouri Events Center." That's BULLSHIT! As far as I'm concerned, as long as it's there it will always be the "BOONE COUNTY FAIRGROUNDS."

NOTE: Well, the location is still there, but the chances of ever holding the Fair there again have been pretty much pissed away by our three glorious Boone County Commissioners. Thanks to the town of Sturgeon for hosting the Fair in 2016, and for inviting it back for 2017. The grounds aren't as big, and it's a long drive for the people in the South end of the county, but sturgeon seems happy to have the opportunity to host the Fair, and the Fair Board doesn't have to deal with the Boone County Commissioners.

Haley Hall
Boone County Journal, Great Reflections, Word of Mouth Catering

Lily Williams
A Show of Hands

Leah Easley
Cedar Creek Therapeutic Riding Center

Taulor Bunch
Allserv Midwest LLC

Nicole Shoop
Bell Excavating

Jordan Curl
Columbia Transmission

Rynda Nichols
Joe Machens Toyota Scion

Morgan Kerr-Totten
Goatsbeard Farm, God's Green Earth, Stanton Farm Fresh Eggs, JW Photography

Queen Candidates

Boone County Fair, 2011. Leah didn't win but she sure looked pretty on the stage.
Columbia Tribune Photo, used with permission.

Kids on the Farm

When I farmed the Frank Hall Place on Bearfield Road I was still working construction and doing my farming at night and on weekends. One Saturday I took my tractor and disk to the Hall Place, and Marcia and the boys followed me. When I pulled in the field they went on down to Pappy's and Mom's to visit for a while before they took me home to get my truck.

Greg was 8 or 9 years old at the time, and as soon as they got out of the car he asked "Grandpap, can I borrow your tractor and go help Daddy disk?" Pappy thought it over a little bit, then said "I 'spect if you're careful that would be all right." Pappy hooked the disk up, then Greg headed up the road towards Hall's, with Marcia following him in the car. When Greg pulled in the field I went over to the gate to see what was going on. When he said he had come to help me disk I showed him what gear to run in, and told him to slow way down while turning with the disk raised.

We disked for a couple of hours before Marcia and Jeff came to get us. When they got there, Greg told Marcia "Momma, nearly everybody that comes down the road stops and stares at me. You'd think they'd never seen a tractor before." Marcia said, "Hon, I'm pretty sure that they've seen tractors before, but they've never seen someone your size driving one."

*   *   *   *   *

When I was a kid, Sis and I and Kenny and John Cavcey used to fish in Clear Creek all the time. We would go wading, float pieces of scrap lumber and call them boats, and do anything else that came to mind. Also, Pappy, Grandpap, and I went to the creek in nice weather to take our baths. The creek was still OK when Greg and Jeff were growing up; occasionally some toys, wooden handled tools, or some plastic watering cans would float down from Woodhaven Home, but the water was still clean. Then somewhere down the line, the Trailer Court north of Nifong Blvd. went from being a nice trailer court to being a ragged-assed rat-hole, and it became home to lots of druggies, and that's when the garbage started floating down the creek.

When Justin was 5 or 6 years old he was with me at Mom's one day, and he wanted to catch craw-dads. He stripped down to his underpants and went wading. He would start in waist deep water, chase the craw-dads towards the bank and then grab one. He was having a ball, and he had waded back into the deeper water to make another pass, when he suddenly bent over and reached down to the bottom of the creek. He straightened up and said, "Look what I found, Paw-Paw," and raised his arm over his head. He was holding a disposable plastic syringe. This was when the AIDS epidemic was at its peak, and when I saw him holding that needle it almost gave me a heart attack. I said "Justin, hold it just exactly like you're holding it now, and wade over here to me. He did, and I checked his hands for scratches, but he hadn't made contact with the needle.

That ended the craw-dad chasing, and that was the last time I let any of the kids go in that creek barefooted. The trailer court has been dozed out, and some supposedly high-end student apartments have replaced it, but there have been two shootings and a couple of drug busts since the place opened, so I'm not sure it's going to be much of an improvement.

* * * * *

The first time I ever saw my Granddaughter Leah with a boy was at a tractor pull in Boonville when she was in Junior High School. It was about time for me to pull, and I was heading for my tractor when I noticed Leah sitting in the third row of the bleachers with a skinny young kid. When I spotted them I didn't say a word, I just stopped and looked from her to him and back again, two or three times. Leah knew I was going to say something, and every time we made eye contact she would give me a nervous little smile. Finally I asked "Leah, is he with you?" When she nodded I looked at the boy and asked, "Do you realize that if you don't treat her right I'll probably kill you?" He didn't say anything, just sat there looking at me, so I stared at him for a moment, then walked away.

Leah said by the time I left, that kid was wondering what the hell kind of family she had. Apparently Greg had left just before I got there, and he had looked at the boy and said "I know so many different ways to kill you that I can't even count them. You'd better watch yourself." The kid couldn't take the pressure, it wasn't very long before Leah had a different boyfriend.

* * * * *

The first time Clint was home on leave when he was stationed in San Diego, he was complaining that no one on his ship understood plain English. He said they didn't know where "over yonder" was, they didn't know when "dreckly" was and his Chief didn't know what Clint meant when he said he would do something when he "got around to it." One day his Chief asked him what he meant by "around to it." Clint said, "It means that I am preparing to complete the task that you have assigned me, at a moment in time that is not at the immediate present." His Chief looked at him and said "Whatever, you damned smart-ass!"

I had a little wooden gift shop souvenir from Branson, MO, about the size of a half dollar. On one side it said "TUIT," and on the other side it said, "You got a round tuit at Branson, MO." I gave it to Clint and told him I couldn't help him with "dreckly" or "over yonder," but at least he could show everyone what "a round tuit" was. Clint told me later his Chief wasn't very impressed. He said, "OK Easley, whatever, but you're still a damned smart-ass!"

I thought about Clint recently, while I was watching "The Marty Stuart Show" on RFD TV. One song had the line "It's a long way from here to over yonder." Clint needed a copy of that song to play for his Chief.

Clint unloading firewood, at least two or three years before he joined the Navy.

*   *   *   *   *

When Greg and Kadi lived in the trailer behind my machine shed, if Justin and Clint weren't with me they were playing in the yard or the machine shed.

My old TR70 New Holland combine was pretty well worn out, and Reese Reeder, who worked for Modern Farm Equipment Co. was here fairly regularly, trying to keep it in one piece. Reese would always talk to the boys when he was here, and they decided he was about the neatest person they'd ever met.

One afternoon Reese was tied up somewhere else, so Norman Schaefer came over to work on the combine. The boys heard some racket out in the shed and they went to investigate. Norman said the boys walked up and looked at him, then Justin asked, "What are you doing to our combine?" When Norman told him the combine was broke and he was fixing it, Justin looked at him and said, "Reese fixes our combine!"

Justin on a "VAC" Case, just a few years after trying to chase Norman off for not being Reese.

Norman said that was the only time a couple of 3 or 4-year-old boys ever tried to run him off the job. He explained to them that Reese was busy and had asked him to come fix it. The boys decided if Reese had asked him to do it, it must be alright, but Norman said they still weren't real happy about him being there. Apparently they finally decided Norman was OK, because later that summer I walked into the shed one afternoon and the boys were sitting on the gravel floor of the shed, with some tools spread out in front of them, playing "Reese and Norman."

*   *   *   *   *

One summer when Greg and Jeff were 8 or 10 years old, Marcia and I took them on the Olivet Church float trip. Everyone pitched tents and camped out, to be ready for an early start the next morning. The adults pretty much all slept in the tents, but most of the kids slept outside in sleeping bags. We'd had a big bonfire and after it had sorta burned down, everyone went to bed.

The next morning several of us had gotten up pretty early, and were thinking about finding some coffee, when someone remarked "I don't know what's burning, but it sure stinks like hell." Someone else looked around and said, "Oh damn, it's that sleeping bag." There were still a lot of coals left from the night before, and Greg had rolled over into them. A couple of us grabbed the bag and drug it out of the fire, then we unzipped it and got Greg out.

It hadn't gotten quite hot enough yet to wake him up, but it wouldn't have been long because the whole bottom of the bag was scorched, and a spot about a foot long was almost burned through. The only thing hurt was the sleeping bag, but I'm sure glad some of us woke up early that morning, or it could have been a whole lot worse.

*   *   *   *   *

Not too long after Gary and Lynn Chandler built their house on Olivet Road, someone started throwing old magazines off the bridge north of their house. One day when Greg and Jeff were visiting at Chandlers, they went exploring with Devin, Darrin, and Dane. They found some magazines and it didn't take those five boys long to figure out there were "nekkid women" in those magazines, and some of them were "doing stuff."

Yeah, they were! The Playboys weren't bad, most of the Penthouse weren't really too bad, but they found a few copies of "Hustler" magazine, and those people were doing things I didn't know how to do. The boys learned real quick everything that two (or sometimes three) people can do, and every position they can do it in.

They had the best stocked tree house in Boone County until Gary found their stash and burned it. Hell, those boys had enough dirty pictures to start a Porn Shop!

*   *   *   *   *

Back in the early 1970's I baled hay a couple of times for J.M. Silvey, on his farm north of Broadway, where the big Hy-Vee Store, fancy church and a bunch of expensive houses are located now. Mr. Silvey raised registered Polled Shorthorn cattle, and Pappy and I bought several bulls from him over the years.

At that time I mowed and baled with a 5000 Ford tractor, and raked with a Farmall "C" (not the same one that Stephen has now). Greg and Jeff were old enough to help (9 or 10) but I did the project during the week when they were in school, so I just switched back and forth from one job to the next, and made it a one-man operation. When the weekend came I was ready to move everything home, so I waited 'til Sunday morning when there would be less traffic, and then headed for the field with the boys.

I hooked the baler behind my truck, put the mower back on the 5000, made sure the rake was out of gear, and then headed toward Broadway with the boys following me. Even though the boys had driven in the field quite a bit I was still a little nervous about this deal. We had to turn left across traffic onto Broadway, then go east all the way through Columbia, going through a couple of 4-way stops, and numerous stop lights. We made it all the way through town with no problems. Jeff might have gone through a couple of stop lights on "pink" because he didn't want to get left behind, and a couple of city cops looked us over pretty good before they smiled and waved as we went by, but we didn't have any problems with traffic.

Sam and Paw-Paw on a Farmall "C"

At that time there wasn't an overpass at Highway 63, there was just a blinking red light and lots of high speed highway traffic. If you see Doris Blackwell sometime, ask her about her experience at that intersection. Anyhow, when we got there I stopped and told the boys to wait while I crossed, then I walked back a couple of times and took both tractors across. Then we headed on home down that narrow, crooked Route WW, and when we got to Olivet Road there luckily wasn't any traffic coming, so we made our left turn off the blacktop with no problems. The boys enjoyed their trip, but I've got to admit it was making me kind of nervous, and I was really glad when we got home. The way traffic is today I'd hate like hell to have to come down Broadway with machinery, even by myself, much less with a couple of 9 or 10-year-old boys following me.

* * * * *

From the time Greg and Jeff were old enough that they could drive a nail, they had a tree house in one of the big Mulberry trees in our back yard. It wasn't a tree house in the sense that it had walls and a roof, it was mostly scrap 2x4's or 1x4's nailed to limbs so they could climb easier, and whenever they came to a good fork they would build a platform big enough to sit on. The older they got the higher in the tree they went.

One day Marcia asked me if I thought their tree house was safe. I said that I couldn't really imagine that it would be. That was the wrong answer! Next thing I knew, I was headed up the tree to check. When I came back down Marcia asked me what I thought about it. I told her it was safe enough as far as I went, but the limbs eventually got too small to support my weight so I quit climbing. I told her that as long as the boys didn't grow too much it would be OK. Before they got too heavy for the limbs, the boys discovered girls and pretty much forgot about the tree house, but they'd had a hell of a lot of fun with it for a long time. Several years later part of the tree went down in a storm, and I had to file my chain saw three times while I was cutting it into firewood. DAMN NAILS!

* * * * *

One evening James Earl, Lee Grant, me and probably 2 or 3 other people were leaning up against a combine in the edge of a cornfield at Greg Michalson's, visiting and drinking a little beer. Tom Grant was 8 or 10 years old at the time, and he was fooling around, just being a pain in the butt. Tom started throwing shelled corn at me, and I told him to stop a couple of times, but he just kept on throwing corn. I finally said "Tom, if you don't quit I'm going to whip your ass." He threw half an ear and hit me in the chest with it, then said "You got to catch me first."

I made one grab at him and missed, then leaned back against the combine again, and acted like I'd forgotten all about him. About 10 minutes later Tom got pretty close, so I grabbed him, dropped to one knee and laid him across my other knee, then whipped his skinny little ass 'til he was hollering stop. When I turned him loose he ran off cussing, and Lee said "Tom, next time Alan says not to do something, you might want to listen to him."

           *   *   *   *   *

Years ago James Earl and David Grant and I were standing in front of James Earl's machine shed when Lee and Tom Grant drove up and stopped. I was wearing a new advertising cap, be it seed corn, chemical or whatever. Tom was a mouthy little fart when he was growing up, and he kept pestering me about my cap. "Easley, I like that cap, I want a cap like that, where'd you get that cap?" I don't remember where I'd gotten the cap, but I finally said from Bourn Feed, just to shut him up.

Apparently I hadn't gotten it from Bourn Feed because the next time Tom was at Bourn's with his dad he asked them for one of the caps, and they told him they didn't have any caps like that. A few days later I saw Lee and Tom, and Tom didn't even say Hi, he just walked up in front of me, looked up and said "EASLEY, YOU'RE A LIEING SON-OF-A-BITCH!"

Normally I would have smacked his ass, or at least had some sort of a comment, but I had no idea what the hell he was talking about, and I was so totally surprised that I just stood there and stared at him. I don't think Tom ever did get one of those caps.

*   *   *   *   *

SORRY VICKI, YOU TOLD THIS FIRST; I'M JUST REPEATING IT.

When Larry McCray was running the hay wagons, one of them broke down one afternoon, and while the boys were waiting for Larry to bring parts they drove back to Blackwell's pond and went skinny-dipping.

Bill happened to walk out of the house, and he asked Vicki what she was doing. She replied, "Just standing on the picnic table." Bill looked again, then said "Well get down off that table, and give me those damn binoculars!"

Vicki was 12 or 13 at the time, and she said she was just kind of curious, and there really wasn't much to see anyhow.

*   *   *   *   *

Paw-Paw with Kaitlan Bradley and Stephen Easley, 1991

Stephen and Sam in front of the old barn on Bearfield Road, Summer 1998

Four Easleys, Clint and Stephen on tractor, Justin and Taylor on ground. This "VAC" was our first restoration.

Tractors and Machinery

One summer when James Earl Grant was in high school he was working for L.D. Baurichter. L.D. was plowing wheat stubble with an M Farmall and a 3-bottom plow, and James Earl was using an H Farmall with a 2-bottom plow.

L.D. was in the lead, and James Earl said that his tractor suddenly stopped, L.D. jumped off and went running across the field, wildly slapping the air with his hat. James Earl stopped, and when L.D. finally circled around to where James Earl was waiting he had several bumble bee stings starting to whelp up. The M was setting in the furrow, running at full throttle. L.D. had slapped at the ignition switch when he jumped off, but he had missed.

James Earl remarked that it probably wasn't good for the tractor to set there and run wide open and maybe they should try to get it shut off. L.D. said it could blow up or run out of gas but he wasn't going back down there with all those bumble bees. James Earl eased his way toward the tractor, and managed to get it shut off without getting stung.

That evening, after the bees had settled in for the night they slipped down to the nest with a little gas and some matches, and solved the bumble bee problem. They moved the M out of the field for the night and went back the next day and finished plowing with no further problems.

* * * * *

When Ansel Pace owned the farm at the northwest corner of Range Line and New Haven Road, he pulled in the field one afternoon around 1:00 pm with his little self-propelled Case combine, to thresh red clover seed. Around 3:00 pm he was turning at the end of the field when J.R. Jacobs came down the road.

J.R. stopped and asked Ansel how the clover was turning out. Ansel said he didn't know, because he hadn't checked yet. He stepped up on the rail so he could see into the bin, then he remarked, "Well, I haven't got any." He walked around the combine with J.R. and they discovered that he had forgotten to close the flap on the bottom of the clean grain elevator. He had cut for two hours, and put all of the seed back on the ground in 6" strips.

*   *   *   *   *

Not long after Marcia and I moved east of town in 1963, I bought my first tractor at a farm auction up towards Hallsville. It was a 1944 DC Case. It wasn't much, but I didn't need much of a tractor back then, just something to drag trees and pull a trash trailer.

Since it was a war time tractor it didn't have a starter, Case had reverted back to a crank and magneto. The tractor had an original tire on one side, worn nearly smooth, and a brand-new tire on the other side with the tread mounted backwards, so it wouldn't out-pull the worn-out tire quite so bad. I kept the old tractor for 3 or 4 years and it pretty much did what I needed it to do.

The tractor had a hand clutch, and when I was done using it I would just pull the clutch back and leave it in gear. When I got ready to start it again I would gently nudge the crank while reaching around the side of the tractor and pulling the choke cable. I would then proceed to give 1/4 turn pulls on the crank. If I had gotten it choked just right it would start on the first, second, or third pull, otherwise it was flooded, and I would have to crank for at least 30 minutes.

One afternoon I choked the tractor, then gave a good pull on the crank. Greg or Jeff, or maybe both of them, had been on the tractor and pushed the clutch forward and shoved the throttle wide open. The damned old thing started on that first pull of the crank, and it wanted a piece of me! If it happened now I'd just say OK, and get squashed, but I was a little quicker back then so I started running backwards. I ran straight back for at least 20 feet before I gained enough room that I could spin to the side and get out of the way. I ran around behind the tractor, jumped on it and pulled the clutch back, then climbed onto the seat and went on with my project. But I'll guaran-damn-tee that was the last time I started that old tractor without first checking the position of the clutch!

*   *   *   *   *

When Doc Kinkead ran his vet practice you always knew exactly what you were paying for. His bills would be itemized; so much for a farm visit, so many miles at 20 cents a mile, so much for chute rental, etc.

When Doc had the place where Marilyn Brown lives now, he slipped into a ditch one day while he was brush hogging. He called me and I went up and pulled him out. After we unhooked Doc asked, "What do I owe you?," as neighbors always do. Instead of the usual "Don't worry about it" I said "Oh, $25.00 for a farm visit, 2 miles at 20 cents a mile, $20.00 tractor rental, $10.00 log chain rental, that's $55.40, total." Doc stood there a moment, then grinned and said, "Oh go to hell, you damn smartass."

*   *   *   *   *

In my first book I told about someone wiring the hand clutch on Tekotte's "50" John Deere, and how it tried to climb a tree with him. I never knew who did it, but Doc Kinkead says it was David Vemer. When you stop and think about all the things those two pulled on each other over the years it seems pretty likely that's who it was.

*   *   *   *   *

One real cold day back in the mid 50's, Virgil Hill built a fire under his 8N Ford tractor to warm it up a little so it would start. Before long the oil and grease that was built up on the side of the engine started burning, and the heat broke the sediment bowl, dumping gas directly onto the fire. In a very short time Virgil was in need of another tractor.

He bought a brand new 1955 "960" Ford from George Russell and used it for several years. When he traded it off at Fullington-Bowen in 1966, I bought it and a new 3-bottom plow from A.F. It was the first decent tractor that I ever owned, and I did a lot of work with it before I traded it to Modern Farm Equipment Co. for a used 5000 Ford in Nov. 1969. That's one old tractor that I wish I had never gotten rid of.

*   *   *   *   *

In my first book when I wrote about Columbia's old time machinery dealers I forgot to mention that Boone County Oil Company handled Co-op tractors and equipment. They were about like the Douglas Feed Co. MM Dealership. If you wanted a tractor or piece of machinery they could order it, and they had a parts book laying on the counter, but that was about as far as it went.

Also, Henry Semon told me that he could vaguely remember a Massey-Harris Dealer on the east side of

North 9th Street, but he said they weren't there very long. Someone told me that Eutsy Johnson owned that dealership.

* * * * *

In the late '70's I was baling hay for Bill Blackwell south of his barn, when one of the knotters on my old baler exploded into a pile of parts. I called Wayne Vandeloecht at Modern Farm Equipment Co., and he took a complete knotter assembly off of a used baler and brought it over. While he was installing it he kept telling me about all of the improvements on the new balers, and trying to convince me that I should swap for one. He had gotten so far as telling me it would only take $2,200.00 to complete the deal. When he got in his truck to leave he asked me if I was going to trade. I said, "Hell no, not for that kind of money, I wouldn't give a dime over $1,800.00." Wayne started to drive off, then he stopped, stuck his head out the window, and asked "You'll get done here today, won't you?" I told him I would if the junky-assed old baler held together. He asked me where I would be baling the next day, and when I told him he waved and drove away. I looked at Bill and asked "B.J., did I just trade balers?" Bill said, "I'm not positive, but I believe maybe you did."

The next day I was baling at Jim Nanson's place, just south of Arno Winkler's. I'd made a couple of rounds when I saw a truck and new baler pulling into the field. We switched balers, robbed the twine out of the old baler and put it into the new one, then Wayne walked beside the baler for a couple of rounds while he made some final adjustments. He stood and watched me bale 2 or 3 more wind rows, then he waved and headed back to Fulton with my old baler. I used that new one for 15 years with no serious problems, until I finally sold it at my farm sale in 1994.

September, 2008. I'm baling hay for Tommy Stewart, with his Ford baler. This is the same model baler I traded to Wayne Vandeloecht, kind of by accident, back in the late 1970's.

*   *   *   *   *

When I farmed the Ruggles Place on Route Z there was usually a steady stream of renters in the "Big House" and the tenant house. One young lady who lived there for a while was particularly well endowed. (She had REALLY big boobs.)

One year I had mowed a bunch of weedy fescue north of the houses, and James Earl Grant was going to round bale it for me. David Grant was in Junior High School at the time, and he and I pulled into the field one morning to start raking. A garden joined the field, and while we were adjusting the rakes the young lady came out of her house in a bathrobe and started picking green beans. I waved, then raked past the garden and headed on around the field.

When I got to the far end of the field I looked back, and David was still raking by the garden. He would rake a little short windrow past the garden, and then turn around and roll it back the other way. I raked on around the field, and James Earl pulled in with the baler just as I got back to the gate.

He watched David for a minute, then walked over and asked, "Alan what in the hell is David doing?" I replied, "Well, he's supposed to be helping me rake hay, but actually he's trying to look down that girl's robe and check out her boobs while she's picking beans." It's a damn good thing there wasn't but two rows of beans, or David might still be there, raking that first windrow back and forth.

*   *   *   *   *

Oscar Elley and his wife lived for many years in the remodeled Jacobs school house just north of I-70 on Route Z. Among other things, Oscar had moved houses for a living, and when he retired he kept all of his equipment. He had a pretty nice little Cat "20" that he still used occasionally. One day he had been working along Route Z when the tractor quit running.

Everett Koester worked for Fabick Equipment Co. as a mechanic, and he was heading south on Route Z in his service truck. Oscar saw that Cat logo on the truck and flagged Everett down. Everett told me it was a real simple fix and 15 minutes after he stopped, the tractor was back running. At that time Fabick charged $40.00 per hour, with a half hour minimum.

Oscar was known to be pretty close with his money, and when Everett told him the bill was $20.00, Oscar threw a fit. $20.00 for 15 minutes? He couldn't believe it.

Everett didn't feel like arguing about it so he thought he would just shame Oscar into paying him. He said, "Well Mr. Elley, if you can't afford $20.00 don't worry about it, I'll just do it for nothing." Oscar smiled from ear to ear and said, "Well thank you young man, I really appreciate that." Everett said that as he drove away without any money he thought to himself, "Well Everett, maybe someday you'll learn to keep your mouth shut."

*   *   *   *   *

May, 1976. Jeff, Alan, and Greg with a new tractor. Oscar wasn't the only one who liked new stuff.

Oscar never saw a piece of machinery that he didn't like, and Mrs. Elley fussed at him quite a bit about buying so much "stuff." Oscar had a nice little Allis-Chalmers "C" that he baled hay with. Pappy told me that when Oscar bought the "C" he didn't want his wife to know about it, so he took it to the back side of the farm and built a stack of loose hay around the tractor.

By the time spring came and the hay was fed, the tractor was filthy and the paint was stained in places from wet hay laying on it all winter. It didn't look anything like a new tractor, so one afternoon Oscar put the battery back in it and drove it up to his barn. Mrs. Elley never did know that Oscar had bought another tractor.

*   *   *   *   *

We don't salvage nearly as many old tractors as we did years ago. It seems like it's a lot more work than it used to be, however, we still latch on to one occasionally. This John Deere "60" was our most recent project. Jeff found it setting in a yard in a subdivision, slowly sinking into the ground.

Jeff and I, and Bill Blackwell, spent well over a half day freeing up the brakes and clutch and getting it loaded, then before we got it home we sold it to Zane Dodge. Zane removed the 3-point hitch assembly to use on another tractor that he was restoring, then he resold the "60." The buyer replaced a tire and worked on the brakes before he resold it. The next owner got it running (roughly) and sold it in a consignment auction. That last buyer had better keep the old tractor, because I think the profit chain is about used up.

A lot of dollars were rolled over in a three-month period on that old piece of scrap iron. No one made very much, but we were all doing our part to stimulate Mr. Obama's economy.

Jeff's "60"

* * * * *

It's always nice to have someone you can go to for an "expert opinion" if you need one. Recently I went to the big town of Roach, MO, to look at a 1755 Oliver. It was one of those "awkward age" tractors, almost too old to use regularly, but not old enough to take to an antique tractor show. It had a heated cab and a front end loader, and I thought that after 71 years maybe a warm cab would be nice when I was feeding cattle and blading snow.

I had talked to the owner on the phone a couple of times, and the day I went to look at the tractor I took Zane Dodge with me to see what he thought about it. We looked it over pretty good, asked several questions, and then we both drove it around some. Zane agreed with me that the old tractor should be able to do everything I needed it to do, and it was probably worth the money.

On the way home Zane was telling me about his latest tractor purchase, a "B" John Deere. He said the more he messed with it the more problems he found, some of them pretty serious. He finally decided to cut his losses, so instead of doing a lot of work and spending a lot of money on the old tractor, and then losing $1,000.00, he took a quick $900.00 loss and got out from under it.

"Expert opinion" my ass! Oh well, we had a damn good visit that afternoon, something we don't do near often enough, anymore.

*   *   *   *   *

When I was a kid a guy owned a small farm on Rock Quarry Road, north of Gregory's Place. His name was Weiker or Wyker, but whenever Pappy spoke of him he called him "Mr. Wackier," because Hale Cavcey told him once that the guy was "Wackier than a bedbug."

Late one spring Hale showed up at our house one day on his 8N Ford and told Pappy that he wanted to lease the tractor to Pappy for the rest of the year, for $1.00. Apparently "Mr. Wackier" had borrowed Hale's tractor and mower for a couple of days. When he brought it home he parked it in the shed, thanked Hale and told him that everything worked fine, and said that he would probably need to borrow it again in a couple of weeks.

The next time Hale looked at his tractor and mower he couldn't hardly believe what he found. The tractor was almost out of gas, it needed to be greased, it was a quart low on oil, the radiator cap was missing, the 3-point hitch lynch pins were gone and had been replaced with bolts that were bent over with a hammer, and several cotter keys were missing and had been replaced with pieces of baling wire. Also, several sections were broken out of the mower sickle, and 2 or 3 guards were completely gone.

August, 1971. Pappy, Karl DeMarce, and 1949 8N Ford. This is the same model tractor that Pappy "Leased" from Hale Cavcey for $1.00 per year.

Hale always had trouble telling someone "no," and he told Pappy that if the tractor was leased out for the summer it would be a lot easier to tell the guy "no" when he wanted to borrow it again. Hale said if he needed to use the tractor he'd tell Pappy a couple of days ahead of time, so we could have it unhitched from whatever piece of equipment we were using.

Pappy "leased" the tractor for a couple of years, 'til Mr. "Wackier" moved away. By then Pappy had kind of got used to having two tractors around, so that fall he bought the "860" Ford that Bill Blackwell owns now, and used it until he passed away in 1982.

*   *   *   *   *

Previously published in "Today's Farmer" and "Antique Power." Used with permission.

Bill Blackwell, me, and Zane Dodge, with Bill's 1957 "860" Ford tractor. Pappy bought this tractor new in November 1957. Bill has owned it since April 1982.

When I was a kid, Pappy and Grandpap farmed with one team which was well past its prime, and an old 8N Ford tractor. In 1957 they bought a new 860 Ford tractor, a three-bottom plow and an eight-foot disk. I didn't think there was enough ground in Boone County to keep me busy, using machinery that big.

The 860 was a lot faster than the old 8N, and I opened it up for a fast run at every opportunity. After a few lectures, I soon learned not to do that unless I was out of sight of everyone else. The first winter we had the tractor there was a lot of snow. I thought it was great fun to lock the inside brake and slide around in circles in the snow. Kids today call it "cutting doughnuts."

One weekend it snowed, warmed up and then turned real cold, leaving a glaze of ice on everything. After we finished feeding, Pappy told me to put the tractor in the shed, and he went to the house. Now was my big chance.

Ice was a lot slicker than snow; this would really be fun! To get to the shed I had to go through two gates, one at a 45-degree angle to the other one. I decided to go through the first one at full throttle, then hit the brake and slide sideways through the second one. It didn't work. I slid sideways all right but not through the second gate. The rear wheel hit the gate post, broke it off and flung it onto the roof of a hog house with part of the gate still attached. Pappy had seen it all through the kitchen window, and by the time I got stopped, he was slipping and sliding down across the lot. When he got there I was off the tractor, and we stood there silently for several moments surveying the damage. Then Pappy used his strongest expression, which I heard fairly regularly when I was a boy: "GOOD GOSH-A-MIGHTY, ALAN!"

When Pappy passed away in 1982, Mom had an auction of his machinery. Bill Blackwell expressed an interest in the tractor, so I took him to Mom's before the sale to let him check it out. After driving it around, he said he thought the lug nuts were loose on the left rear wheel, because it seemed to have a wobble in it. I mumbled something to the effect: "It's not loose; just got sprung a little; long time ago; don't worry about it."

Bill bought the tractor, still uses it and if you pass by on the road when he's working you can still see that wheel wobbling its way across the field.

*   *   *   *   *

Previously published in "Today's Farmer." Used with permission.

When I was a kid Joe Crane had a pretty decent little Farmall "C," however he still did most of his work with a team, because he said it didn't make much sense to buy gas for a tractor when "The dad-blamed horses have to eat anyway."

I wouldn't want to say Joe was tight, but he was sure 'nuff cautious with his money. Meda was even more cautious that he was, and she kept a pretty close watch on the purse strings. Women didn't wear pants back then, but if they had Meda would have damn sure worn the pants in that family.

One spring Joe somehow convinced her that he had to have new tires for his tractor. He drove it to town to save the cost of a service call and had four new tires mounted. Joe always kept his tractor in an old log cabin behind his house that had one end partially sawed out to allow access. When Joe got home with his tractor he headed straight for the cabin. I don't know why it was there, but driven about 3/4 of the way into the end of one of the logs was a twenty penny spike nail. Joe had been snagging his britches on that nail for years without doing anything about it, but that day as he pulled the tractor into the cabin he decided to drag the rear tire on the nail, and bend it over out of the way.

It didn't bend! The nail poked through the sidewall and ripped a 6" gash in that brand-new tire. Joe waited until Meda was out in the yard, then he called the Co-op and told them to tear up the check he had just written, and add the cost of another tire and a service call onto the bill. He then told them "Do NOT come out to the farm until I call you." One afternoon when Meda was at an Extension Club meeting, Joe called them and they came out and installed another tire. Everyone in the neighborhood knew what had happened but no one said a word, and luckily for Joe, Meda never did find out about that extra tire.

* * * * *

The equipment I grew up with was pretty small by today's standards, but back in the late 1940's, 50's and early 60's it was pretty much average. Bottom farmers had bigger equipment, and a few really big hill farmers did also, but most farms got by with much less than we had.

Momma, Sarah Middleton, and Pappy's Ford combine, early 1960's.

Pappy's Wood Brothers corn picker, early 1960's. Actually it was a snapper; they were cheaper, and the hogs didn't care that at least 25% of the ears still had some shuck on them.

We were the only farm in the neighborhood with two tractors, an 860 and an 8N Ford. We also had the only combine; it evolved over the years from a 4 1/2' cut Case to a 5' cut Case, and finally to a 6' cut Ford. Pappy cut wheat for everyone in the neighborhood with those little combines. By the time Pappy quit crop farming in the mid 1960's, most people were starting to use self-propelled combines, though by today's standards those little 10' cut machines look pretty insignificant. Two-row mounted pickers were also becoming the norm, instead of the one row pull type picker that Pappy had.

*   *   *   *   *

After Dr. Nifong's farm became the property of Woodhaven Home it started going downhill, because they didn't want to spend any money to maintain the ground. Since the ground is now completely covered with 4-plexes and student apartments I don't suppose it really mattered in the long run. One spring Pappy asked the Woodhaven Administration if they would consider liming the farm, and they informed him that liming farm ground wasn't part of their mission. Pappy pretty much informed them that renting ground that wouldn't raise a decent crop wasn't part of his mission. When he left that day they had agreed to hire him to sow the farm in Fescue.

Pappy told me that when he walked out of the Woodhaven Office that morning it felt like a load had been lifted from his shoulders. If he had kept on crop farming he would have needed to trade some equipment before too long, and he really didn't want to keep crop farming long enough to wear out another set of machinery. As it was, he traded the old Ford Combine to George Russell for a new post hole digger, sold the one row Wood Brothers corn picker to Billy Roddy, and eventually sold the old 8N Ford tractor and a few pieces of unnecessary equipment to Henry Semon at Henderson Implement Co.

After that Pappy just concentrated on his cows. He did mow and rake his own hay for several years, until his emphysema got so bad that he couldn't stand the dust, and after that I took care of his hay and his cattle for him, until I finally bought his cows and rented the farm in the late 1970's.

*   *   *   *   *

Back in the mid 1980's I used to help James Earl Grant mow sudan for the Smith Brothers in the Perche Creek bottom west of Scott Blvd. There were two ways to get there; WW to Broadway, then through Columbia on Broadway and south on Scott Blvd, or Nifong Blvd. to Scott Blvd., then north on Scott. Neither was much fun, even 35 years ago, but I'd really hate like hell to try to get there with a hay-bine the way traffic is today. Larry Traxler is now farming that bottom, so it's still possible to get there, but I'm glad he's the one doing it instead of me.

*   *   *   *   *

The first time I traded tractors with Wayne Vandeloecht at Modern Farm Equipment Co. in Fulton, MO, was in November 1969. In June 2014, I traded lawn mowers with his son, Donnie, at Modern Farm Equipment Co. in Fulton, MO.

That's not bad, doing business with the same family owned dealership for 45 years. Maybe in 2019 I'll swap mowers again, just so we can call it an even 50 years.

*   *   *   *   *

Can't start 'em too young. Paw-Paw and Clint, 1988

James Earl Grant checking our projects, February 2002.

Ready to go pulling, April 2005.

Me pulling at Russellville, April 2005

Schools and School Boards

I don't know exactly how long it's been since 7th and 8th grade boys served as janitors in Boone County Schools, but I'll guaran-damn-tee it's been quite a while. That tradition ended when the last one room school closed its doors for good.

When I was in grade school the janitor's job was one of the best ways there was for a kid to make some spending money. The job always went to one or two of the oldest boys in school, so it helped if the enrollment was kind of small, which it usually was. And it didn't hurt anything if your Dad was on the School Board, no one worried very much about nepotism back then.

I started my two-year career as school janitor when I was in the 7th grade at Grindstone School. The first year I shared the job with John Cavcey, who was in the 8th grade. Our dads both happened to be on the School Board at that time. The job consisted of unlocking the school each morning and stirring up the fire, a few minutes each day checking the furnace and shoveling coal, about 45 minutes each afternoon sweeping out the mud and crud, and at least one afternoon each month mopping and waxing the floor. Then at the end of the month we each got a check for ten dollars. Who could ask for anything better than that?

We always took turns stoking the furnace because to get to the basement steps we had to pass through the small, cramped area that served as a school kitchen. By the middle of the morning there was usually some dessert that was ready to eat and the cook, Mildred Howard, was always willing to hand us a sample as we passed through. At lunch time we took turns pumping the old pitcher spout pump so that everyone could pretend to wash their hands. Grindstone was fixed up pretty fancy, the cistern was at the corner of the school, but it was piped into a holding tank in the basement. The pump was mounted over a large tin sink upstairs, and it pumped water from the tank into the sink. The sink drain ran through the wall and dumped into a puddle outside. If someone was mad at the janitor that puddle made it possible for them to track mud inside, even in the middle of a drought. And some of the little assholes did it, just to see if they could make John and I cuss a little bit.

We had a lot of trouble keeping the fire lit all night. When it went out it would take two or three hours the next morning to get the school really warmed up good. John and I had gotten pretty tired of our teacher, Hazel Moreau, fussing at us about the school being cold so we kept adding a little extra coal each afternoon. One really cold winter day we decided that the fire was not going to go out again. We kept stuffing coal into the old furnace until we finally said "There, by God, that son-of-a-bitch won't go out tonight." It didn't!

About 1:00 a.m. our phone rang and Pappy was informed that the school was on fire. The furnace had gotten red-hot and ignited a box of trash that we had carelessly left sitting a little too close. (Actually, a whole bunch too close.) There were no rural Fire Departments back then, but since it was a school building Fire Chief Max Woods and the Columbia Fire Department made an exception to their policy and came out to the country to fight the fire. A bucket brigade was set up for about 300 to 400 yards, as water was moved one bucket at a time from Earl Moss' pond and dumped into the cistern, so the firemen would have some type of water supply, however poor it might be. They did an excellent job considering what they had to work with, and they finally got it out, but about all that was left was a brick shell with a roof.

The district was in the process of planning New Haven School to replace the seven one room schools, so the old building wasn't rebuilt. Forrest and Jim Warren hastily installed glass in the doors and windows of the old abandoned Carlisle School building about eight miles away at the corner of WW and Rolling Hills Road. An LP gas furnace was installed and the old building was used for a year and a half, until the new school was opened in the fall of 1956.

My entire 8th grade class, 1956. Marilyn Elder, teacher Hazel Moreau, and me, in front of the coal shed at the old Carlisle School, after Grindstone burned.

When the seven one room schools finally got moved into the new building things became more modern, and a full-time janitor was hired. John and I had the privilege of being some of the last schoolboy janitors in Boone County.

*   *   *   *   *

When I was a kid, Grindstone School always had a pie supper each year as a fund raiser. The women and girls would bring pies, or occasionally a box supper, and Charlie Cunningham, Rueben Jacobs, Floyd Kemper and later Bandy Jacobs, would auction the pies to the highest bidder.

It was supposed to be anonymous, but if you had a sweetie she'd let you know ahead of time which pie was hers, and of course the men knew what their wives had brought because there was a pretty good chance they had carried it in from the car. Most pies brought 25 or 50 cents, with a few going for up to a dollar. Once in a while several men would gang up on someone, and make him pay 2 or 3 dollars for his wife's pie, but it was all in fun and the money went to purchase supplies that the school needed.

The first year after New Haven School opened there were lots of things that needed to be bought, and the pie supper sort of got out of hand. Billy Boyce ran most of the pies up to 10 or 15 dollars. Occasionally someone would dump a pie on Billy at that price, but most men went ahead and bought their wives' pies, even if they were a little pricy. I was bidding on Emily Short's pie, and Billy made sure it cost me $15.00. I was working for Carver Walkup on Sundays', making $10.00 a week, and that was normally enough to keep me in gas, Camel cigarettes and Pepsi's for a week, so $15.00 for a pie kind of cramped my style for a while.

The next year I just stayed away from the pie supper, and several other people did too. It wasn't over two or three years after that 'til the school dropped the pie supper and went to a chili supper, where you knew what it was going to cost before you ever sat down. The old 50 cent to $1.00 pie suppers were fun, but when they got so expensive that it hurt, the fun wore thin pretty quick.

*   *   *   *   *

When I was in High School, the Pla-Boy Drive-in, on Business Loop 40 just east of Hickman High, was the place to go after movies, ballgames, or whatever. Lots of high school kids went there, some college students, and a sprinkling of adults who were just looking for a good place to eat.

Three or four couples could come in one car, park and order a couple of cokes, and stay for an hour or more without being hassled. The management would make a head check occasionally, and as long as they could see everyone's heads they didn't bother anyone. I don't remember whose car we were in, but one evening we pulled in the Pla-Boy with five couples in one car. Marcia and I were in the backseat with two other couples. It was pretty close quarters back there but we were getting by. I encountered a smooth, warm arm, so I started putting a little love-rub on it with my thumb. We were so snuggled up that my thumb was actually the only thing that I could move. After a few moments the girl sitting next to Marcia, I think it was Judy Rae Morris, said "Alan that feels really good, but I think you've probably got the wrong arm." I told you it was pretty crowded in that backseat!

*   *   *   *   *

When Grindstone, "Colored" Grindstone, Deer Park, Turner, Carter, Carlisle and Robnett Schools combined to form New Haven School in 1956, each of the schools turned boxes of records over to New Haven. Several of the schools had burned and been rebuilt over the years, but many of the records went back to the late 1800's or early 1900's. These records were carefully stored in the vault at the new school.

I was on the New Haven School Board when we were annexed into the Columbia School District. We met for lunch with the Columbia Board members and Administrators, and told them several things that we thought might help with the transition, one of the things being that any old records they might need were in the vault. However, they didn't really seem to care what we had to say about anything. They were rather condescending, and had the attitude "Let's feed these damn farmers, maybe it will make them feel better about losing their school, and they'll go away and leave us alone." I've damn sure left them alone, I've voted against everything they've asked for since then and I'll keep on doing that, I'm pretty good at holding a grudge.

One of the things that Columbia did, in their infinite wisdom, was throw away all of the one room school records to make more room in the vault for their important stuff. In the 1980's I got a phone call one evening from a lady in Vermont or maybe Rhode Island, I don't remember which. She asked me if I had attended Grindstone School around 1950, and if my Dad had served on the School Board. When I told her yes, she identified herself as Vera Haley, and said she had taught for one year at Grindstone. I knew exactly who she was because a couple of months earlier I had run across a box full of old school pictures, and one of them was a group picture from 1949/1950, with Vera Haley as teacher. She told me that she had filed for her teacher's retirement and that she needed the one year at Grindstone to qualify. She had called the Columbia School District and they told her they had never heard of Grindstone School. I told her to tell them that Grindstone became part of New Haven, and that the records were in the New Haven vault. That's when we discovered that all of the old records had disappeared.

My sister, Virginia, had an extra copy of the school picture and she sent it to Mrs. Haley, along with a notarized letter stating that she had attended Grindstone School in 1949/1950, and Mrs. Vera Haley had been the teacher. That was all it took to get her retirement approved, but it's still a shame that all of those years of Boone County school history were destroyed, just to make more room in the vault!

This is the picture that helped Mrs. Haley get her teacher's retirement.

*   *   *   *   *

When Bill Blackwell, Larry McCray and I were on the New Haven School Board, we were always on the lookout for a qualified candidate to run for the Board. One year we had talked it over and decided that Gene Brown needed to be on the Board. One afternoon around 6:00, Bill and I pulled in Gene's driveway. He said the first thing he heard after we got out of my truck was "Brown, where's the damn beer?" Gene wasn't a beer drinker, but he said there was some stale beer in his refrigerator. We didn't wait for him to go after it, I went and got it myself and handed one to Bill, then we sat down out in the yard.

Gene said there was no way in hell that the two of us together could possibly be up to anything good, and he asked what we were doing. Bill told Gene that we were sitting in his yard drinking his beer and when we finished we had some papers for him to sign so he could file as a school board candidate. Gene said, "Oh no, no, hell no!" We just kept sitting there, and occasionally Bill or I would mention the School Board. Around dark the mosquitoes started biting, and pretty soon Gene said, "You all can go home, go to hell, or go wherever you want to go, but I'm going in the house and get away from these damn mosquitoes." Bill told him that since we weren't done with our business we'd just go in with him. We sat and visited with them while they ate supper, then around 10:00 Marilyn said she was going to bed, so we told her goodnight and continued sitting. Anytime we tried to talk about the school board Gene would turn the TV up a little louder. Just before 11:00 Gene turned the TV off and said he had to work the next day, so he was going to bed. He told us to turn the lights out and lock the door when we left.

We weren't done with our business, so we looked around and found some snacks, then we just kept sitting. Around 12:30 Gene got back up and came in the living room. He said, "You assholes are talking so damn loud that there's no way in hell I can go to sleep. If I sign those damn papers will you go home?" We assured him we would, so he signed them and we left. Gene told everyone he talked to that he didn't want to be on the School Board and his opponent did so everyone should vote for his opponent. It didn't work, when it was all over Gene had won by two votes. Despite the fact that he didn't want the job he made a right decent board member, and he wound up actually enjoying the experience. Gene was still on the Board when we finally got sucked into the Columbia School District.

*　　*　　*　　*　　*

When I was a senior at Hickman High during 1959/1960, Conrad Stawski was my English teacher. He taught Composition and Grammar, one semester of each. You've probably noticed that most of the grammar didn't stick with me, and some of you might say that I haven't done a hell of a lot with the composition part, but I've had a bunch of fun with it over the past fifty-some years.

Mr. Stawski was white headed, and I thought he was practically an antique in 1960, so you can imagine how surprised I was when our boys started coming home from Rock Bridge in the late 1970's, talking about "Mr. Stawski." I had one of the boys ask him his first name and when they told me I realized that he was still going strong, nearly 20 years later. I had several good visits with him at school functions while the boys were at Rock Bridge. He told me there had been too many changes in the school system to suit him, he didn't like most of them, and he couldn't hardly wait to retire.

I talked to him a couple of times after I started selling a few magazine articles in the early 1990's, and I thanked him once for getting me interested in writing. He told me when one of his former students was successful he took absolutely no credit for it, he said "That way, if one of my former students becomes a serial killer, I don't have to take any blame for that." He was really a pretty neat old man.

*   *   *   *   *

When I was in Hickman no one realized that smoking would eventually kill you, and there wasn't the social stigma attached to it that there is today. The teachers had a lounge that they smoked in, and students could smoke anywhere on the school grounds. In really bad weather they let us smoke inside the south vestibule. Occasionally Mr. Steer would stick his head in and say, "Pretty smoky boys, you'd better open the door for a minute."

Mr. Stawski couldn't make it through a whole class period without a cigarette so he would slip out to the teacher's lounge for a quick smoke every day. Before he would leave he would look at his watch and announce, "I'll be back in exactly five minutes, and I don't want to catch anyone smoking in class when I get back." As soon as he left, 3 or 4 of us would open a window and smoke a quick cigarette, but we always finished in time. Mr. Stawski never caught us smoking in class when he got back.

*   *   *   *   *

When I was a sophomore at Hickman we had a teacher who I thought was uglier than a cake of homemade lye soap, but apparently he looked better to the girls. Anyhow, a couple of years later he got caught messing with some of them and got his ass fired.

Some things never change, there's always some son-of-a-bitch trying to take advantage of who he is or what he does!

*   *   *   *   *

When the boys were in Rock Bridge High School, and Norm Beal was living with us, we kind of had a "revolving door" policy at the house. Marcia was working at MU and didn't get home 'til around 5:30, and I was farming so I might or might not be home in the afternoon, just depending on what kind of project I had going on at the time.

One afternoon when I pulled in the driveway around 4:30, I noticed two cars that weren't familiar, but Greg's truck wasn't there and Jeff's and Norm's Mustangs were gone too. The garage door was open, so I walked in through the garage and went into the kitchen. Three boys and three girls were sitting at the kitchen table and I had never seen any of them before. When I said, "What's up, guys?" one of the girls replied "Oh, we came to see Jeff and Norm, but they're not home yet, so we're just eating a snack while we're waiting on them." They damn sure were! They all had a plate with a sandwich on it, and lunch meat, cheese, pickles, lettuce, mustard, mayonnaise, potato chips and Fritos were scattered around on the table, along with a jug of milk and a couple of different flavors of sodas.

I said "Well, I just came by the house to pick up something, I guess the boys will be home before long. Put your dishes in the dishwasher when you get done eating, and make yourselves at home." They assured me they would, so I got in my truck and headed back down the road, leaving the house in the hands of strangers. The boys had some pretty rowdy friends when they were in high school, but they were all honest, and it's a damn good thing because everyone the boys ran around with knew where the house key was hidden, and they all pretty much came and went when they wanted to. A couple of bottles of "Jim Beam" sprung a leak once, but that's the only thing we ever missed.

Boone County Food

In my first book, I included the following story about Grandpap congratulating Grandma on her pie crust. Several people asked me why I didn't include her pie crust recipe in the book. I didn't think about it, that's why, so I'm reprinting the story here, along with the recipe, and it is "Good Crust, Kate."

*   *   *   *   *

Grandpap finished every meal with something sweet. Not just most meals, EVERY meal. At breakfast it was usually a hot buttered biscuit with jelly or syrup, at dinner and supper it could be cake, pie, cookies, pudding, maybe mom's sweet rice, or a bowl of strawberries or sliced peaches with thick cream. He liked it all, but pie was his favorite. Actually, pie crust was his favorite, the filling didn't have to be anything to brag about as long as the crust was good.

I don't remember Grandpap every commenting on how good an entire slice of pie was, but he was always ready to brag on the crust. I can still hear him today; he would finish his pie, place the silverware on his empty plate, then look at Grandma and say, "Good Crust, Kate."

*   *   *   *   *

Pie Crust
Kate Cheavens Easley

Short one cup lard
3 cups flour
1 teaspoon salt
about ½ cup cold water

Put lard in bowl, sift dry ingredients and add. Mix until it looks creamy. Add water slowly, using just enough to hold the dough together. It should come clean from the sides of the bowl. This should be enough for 2 pies. If it doesn't come out that way for you, just double the recipe. Bake any extra in a small pan with cinnamon, butter, and sugar for the children to eat.

---

*   *   *   *   *

Marcia didn't like gooseberry pie; therefore, she didn't like to make gooseberry pie, but she usually made me one or two a year anyhow.

I'm not real particular about what I eat, so after my Baby died, I was getting along pretty good on fried meat, eggs, peanut butter sandwiches and cornbread, but I was getting hungry for a gooseberry pie. My "some sort or another of a cousin," Maggie Cheavens Danley, baked me a big old gooseberry pie one day, and her and her sweet Momma, Edy, brought it out to the house. Damn, it was good! It lasted me exactly two days. I called her and told her, "Good Crust, Kate."

A couple of months later, I mailed Maggie 3 cans of gooseberries. That way, if she wakes up some morning and decides she wants to bake me another pie, she won't have to run all over town looking for gooseberries. Damn, I'm thoughtful.

(About 2 weeks later, Maggie brought me another gooseberry pie. Maggie's pretty thoughtful, too.)

*   *   *   *   *

My favorite pie is gooseberry, but there's nothing wrong with cream pie, either. If you wake up some morning and decide it's a good day not to worry about calories, fat content or cholesterol, make this pie, it's just as good as gooseberry, but in a totally different way.

Cream Pie
Kate Cheavens Easley

1 cup sugar
3 heaping Tablespoons flour
3 Tablespoons butter
1 teaspoon Vanilla
2 cups cream
1/3 teaspoon salt
Unbaked pie shell

Mix sugar and flour; mix in butter; add cream and flavoring (it is all right if little lumps of butter are floating around in the mixture. Pour into unbaked pie shell. Bake at 450 degrees for 15 minutes, reduce heat to 350 degrees and bake until done, about 40 minutes more.

Three notes on this pie:
1) Grandma always baked it in a heavy glass pie plate.
2) She used really heavy cream from our own cows, but whipping cream from the store works okay.
3) Make two of 'em, 'cause one won't last.

*   *   *   *   *

When Marcia was fixing supper, she would usually get everything else done, and then she would come into the family room and sit while whatever was in the oven finished cooking. Our little dog, Skeeter, knew the sound of the timer, and when that bell rang, he would spin around in circles three or four times, then run into the kitchen and dance around between the stove and the table, waiting for us to come and eat.

*   *   *   *   *

I picked up a jar of Smucker's Red Plum Jam at the store the other day. The label said 26 servings, 50 calories per serving. Whoever wrote that label didn't grow up on homemade jam, jelly and preserves. Mom and Grandma put the stuff up in pint jars, and there would always be two or three flavors on the table at every meal. We would put a pile of jelly on our plates the size of a normal vegetable serving, and however much would lay on a knife long enough to transfer it to a biscuit made one bite.

Those 26 servings of Smuckers Red Plum Jam? Made me 4 servings, and the last one was a little bit skimpy. Thirteen hundred calories per jar, that's three hundred twenty-five per serving. By the time you eat some sausage and eggs, and three or four biscuits, that makes for a right decent breakfast. Or supper.

*   *   *   *   *

Cornbread and buttermilk makes one of the best down-home, stick-to-your-ribs meals that you can get. It's pretty simple, too. Just crumble some stale cornbread in a bowl or big glass, and pour on some buttermilk. Pretty decent eating!

*   *   *   *   *

When I was a little kid, Pappy and Mom rented a locker at Columbia Ice and Storage to keep meat, vegetables, and fruit. However, I can barely remember a couple of times at hog-killing when Mom and Grandma canned meat. They fried sausage in balls, and put it in crocks and covered it with hot lard, and then stored it in the cellar. It would keep for a long time sealed in that grease. The tenderloins were pressure canned in glass jars, but I have no idea how they prepared it. Betty Glenn told me that she has canned tenderloin and sausage. She probably knows more about it than anyone around.

We nearly always had sweet-breads for supper on butchering night, and brains and eggs for breakfast the next morning. I don't know if I could even find the sweet-breads in a gut pile anymore, but they're definitely worth the trouble it takes to find them. Damn, they're good eating.

*   *   *   *   *

After Marcia died, I found out that my cooking left a lot to be desired, but I'm getting better. I can fry meat and eggs, bake canned biscuits, make some pretty decent cornbread, hard boil eggs, and make a pretty good pot of beans and country ham. I'm getting pretty good with desserts, too. I don't make them, but I haven't found a package of store-bought cookies yet that I can't open.

*   *   *   *   *

Grandpap didn't eat beef. He thought that you raised hogs to eat and cattle to sell. He ate pork three times a day, seven days a week, the only exception being Sunday morning when we had pancakes. Country cured ham, shoulder, bacon and sausage were his favorites, but he also liked boiled backbone with sauerkraut or turnips, and he liked tenderloin if it was sliced thin and fried 'til it started to get crispy around the edges. He would eat a little pork roast or pork steak, but he really thought that was a waste of good meat that could have been cured or ground into sausage. I guess all of that salt and grease finally got to him, because he had a stroke and passed away when he was 98.

The last couple of years that Grandpap was alive, he had kind of lost his taste. One evening mom had fixed hamburgers for supper. She had put a little plate of cold bacon on the table so Grandpap would have some meat, but the first thing he did was fork a hamburger onto his plate. No one said anything as we watched him eat it. He took another one, and when he was about half done with it, he said, "Margaret, this sausage could sure use some more seasoning." Mom replied, "Pap, those aren't sausage, they're hamburgers."

Grandpap didn't say a word, he just took his fork and started nudging that half a hamburger toward the edge of his plate. Eventually he pushed it far enough that it tipped off his plate onto the table. Grandpap didn't say another word, he just finished the rest of his supper. He'd eaten 1½ patties of what he thought was bland sausage, but he didn't even want that last half a patty on his plate after he found out it was hamburger.

*   *   *   *   *

When I was a kid, chicken, rabbit and squirrel were all handled the same way; soaked overnight in salt water, then rolled in flour and fried in a lot of lard until good and brown. It makes Colonel Sanders chicken look 2nd class.

Marcia's fried chicken was even better than what I was raised on. She seasoned it with lemon pepper, and it was so good, I'd almost founder every time she fixed fried chicken.

*   *   *   *   *

Mom and Grandma had a love affair with cast iron skillets and lard. Country ham, sausage, bacon, chicken, rabbit, squirrel, pork chops, tenderloin, pork steak, hamburger, steak, mountain oysters, hogs-head pudding, potatoes, eggs, cornbread, green tomatoes, it was all fried in lard or bacon grease, in a cast iron skillet.

I'm going to die from something eventually, and I think I'd just as soon it be from fried food and lard, at least I'll be well fed.

*   *   *   *   *

Apparently the latest thing that I'm supposed to like is grass-fed beef. Bull's Ass! I grew up on grass-fed beef, and about all I can say for it is "It's meat." It takes at least 90 days of corn to fatten a calf and marble the meat, and if it's not plenty fat and well marbled, you're better off eating venison, it tastes about like grass-fed beef and it's free. Grass-fed beef fills you up, but it doesn't have the rich flavor that beef should have, and it's sure 'nuff not tender.

When I was a kid, I always knew when we were going to have steak for supper. It didn't matter where you were in the house, you could hear whomp, whomp, whomp, whomp, as Momma pounded the steaks with the edge of a heavy plate. Then she would flip them over, turn them 90 degrees, and then whomp, whomp, whomp, whomp again, on the other side. After Mom got done beating the hell out of them, and sprinkling them with "Adolph's

Meat Tenderizer" the steaks were reasonably tender, but they still tasted like grass-fed beef.

I'm fine with other people eating lean meat if that's what they want to do, but I want an inch of waste fat around the edge of my steak while it's cooking. It's not really wasted, the old dogs need to eat, too, and they don't seem to mind fat meat. I don't really like lean hamburger either. 70%/30% is plenty lean enough. Any less fat than that and it won't hardly fry without putting a half a stick of butter in the skillet to get it started. Hamburgers taste good fried in butter, but you might just as well grind up a little more fat and make them right to begin with.

$$* \qquad * \qquad * \qquad * \qquad *$$

When the boys were growing up, Marcia never knew how many people she would have to feed at supper time. Randy and Brent Blackwell might be there, Kevin Brown, one, two or three of the Chandler boys, maybe some girls just for variety, and anyone else who might be around.

Beef Stroganoff was one of Marcia's main dishes if she realized there were going to be extra mouths to feed. She'd just cook an extra package of noodles, and brown another pound or two of hamburger. No one ever left hungry. It's not one of the old-time recipes that I grew up on, but it sure is good.

Hamburger Stroganoff

From a magazine—tweaked by Marcia

Brown 1 pound of hamburger in shortening or oil, with salt & pepper and a chopped up onion. Drain off most of the grease when done. Stir in a can of condensed mushroom soup and a small can of mushrooms with liquid. Simmer for 5 minutes. Blend in a cup of sour cream, heat but don't boil. Dump over a pot of cooked noodles and stir. Sprinkle with parsley flakes. Serves 4.

Marcia would usually double or triple the recipe.

The original recipe called for making little bitty hamburger patties, but when we had a table full of hungry teenagers, we ate it faster than you could make little patties, so Marcia just crumbled it like Chili meat.

*   *   *   *   *

Ever since Jeff and Jean got married, Jean has always brought pecan pies to family dinners. Since Marcia died we don't do big meals here anymore, but where ever the meal is, when Jean gets there, she puts one pie in my truck so that I'll have pie when I get home, and she takes one inside for the meal.

And that girl damn sure makes good pecan pies!

Marcia's Groundhog

Marcia didn't ever go hunting with us. She didn't have a problem with other people hunting, and she definitely wasn't afraid to shoot a gun, but there were other things she would rather do with her time, so she didn't waste any of it hunting.

One Saturday morning, she called me at MFA and she had a sparkle in her voice when she started talking. She said, "Hon, when you get home, you need to carry this dead groundhog off somewhere before it starts stinking." When I asked what dead groundhog, she casually replied, "The one I just shot." I asked where he was and she told me out by the ham building. I said, "Where were you standing, and what did you shoot him with?" She replied "Oh, I was in the west door of the family room, and I shot him with your .22 revolver. He was sitting up and looking around, and I figured he'd go to the garden next, so I shot him." I said, "My God, Babe, that's 40 yards, how many times did you shoot at him?" She said, "Just once, he fell down and didn't

Marcia with my .22 revolver and her dead groundhog.

move, so I figured he was dead." He was definitely dead. She had made a perfect head shot with a .22 revolver at 40 yards.

My baby never did admit that she probably wouldn't ever be able to make that shot again, but she sure had a lot of fun telling the women she worked with about her big groundhog hunt.

Hunters and Hunting

When Greg and Jamie lived in Columbia, Greg was the only person in their neighborhood who hunted. Depending on the season he would dress squirrels, rabbits, or coons, and clean fish on the carport, and in November he would always have 3 or 4 deer hanging there.

Most of the neighbors didn't mind, but one woman who lived south of them was a vegan. She thought eating meat was horrible, but killing it yourself was even worse. She told anyone who would listen that Greg was the "neighborhood barbarian." Anytime she passed the house when Greg and the boys were dressing game Greg would always wave at her with a dead squirrel, deer liver, or fish head in his hand.

Clint with some dead deer. How about that, vegan lady?

That old gal wasn't the least bit sorry when Greg and Jamie sold their house and moved to the country.

*   *   *   *   *

I've hunted all my life, my sons hunt, my daughter-in-law Jamie hunts, my grandkids hunt, and I have a lot of respect for most hunters. However, a few of them ought to be knocked in the head with a club and stomped under a brush pile.

If you dumb bastards need to get your dogs through a fence and you're not big enough to lift them over, walk 'til you find a gate. Don't cut my fence, you assholes. When the two barbwires are still intact, and the woven wire is cut to within a foot of the ground and folded back out of the way, it's pretty obvious why you did it.

Pricks like you are the reason that hunters have more trouble every year getting permission to come on someone's property. You ruin it for everyone else, I'll bet your Momma's are really proud of you!

*   *   *   *   *

During the late 1960's, four black men stopped at our house one Saturday afternoon. They told me they were from St. Louis, and they said they had been driving all day trying to find a place where someone would let them go rabbit hunting. Rabbits were thick that year, so I showed them where my property lines were and told them to be careful, then I walked out to the mailbox while they headed for the brush.

Before I got back to the house I heard shots. I stepped around the corner of the house and they were standing in our garden, lined up about 3 feet apart, blasting away. I hollered "What in the hell are you doing?" When they said that there were rabbits everywhere, I said "That's part of my damn yard, and that's my boys' sandbox, about 30 feet from where you're standing. If you dumbasses can't wait 'til you're out of my yard to start shooting, get your in your car and get the hell out of here!"

They apologized, but I was already pissed so I told them to get gone. They weren't very happy about it, but they took their three rabbits and left. It's hard to believe they were so impatient that they started shooting while they were still in the yard. It's no wonder no one wanted to let them hunt.

*   *   *   *   *

Occasionally over the years I would kill a groundhog out by the shed. George Williams loved groundhogs, and he was always glad to come get them. The last time I called George he said he just didn't feel like coming after a groundhog and dressing it. I knew then that age was finally catching up with George. He passed away not long after that. I miss him, he was a fine gentleman.

Before his knees got bad, George's son, Ed, used to come out hunting several times a year, usually for rabbits, but he came coon hunting once in a while, and generally had pretty good luck.

One of George's grandsons, Chris, has been trapping the creek back of our house the last couple of winters. You don't have to talk to Chris very long to know that he spent quite a bit of time around George. He's a gentleman, too, just like his Granddad was. Chris, you're welcome to trap here anytime.

*   *   *   *   *

During the late 1980's I was driving around on Greg Michalson's farm one morning looking for a steer that was missing, when I noticed a big old red hound dog coming slowly across the bean stubble. The ground was frozen and that old dog's feet were sore, he was picking his spots very carefully. I called him, then squatted down next to my truck and started talking to him.

He was pretty cautious but he slowly worked his way closer. I got some snack crackers out of the truck and ate a couple of them while he watched, then I offered him one. He eased up to me and cautiously took it, then eagerly ate the rest of them. I opened the truck door and invited him inside. He jumped in, turned around 3 or 4 times, laid down and gave a big sigh and went to sleep. He was wearing a collar with a phone number on it, so when I got home I left him in the truck while I went in the house and called the number. When I asked the man who answered if he had lost a hound, he replied that he had lost two of them the night before. When I told him that I had one of them sleeping in my truck he said he appreciated it, and said to tell him where I lived and he would come take his hound off my hands.

I started my directions with "Go about 5 miles east of town on Route WW, then _ _ _." He interrupted me and said "Whoa, just a minute, where are you starting from?" When I told him Old Highway 63 and Broadway there was a moment of silence, then he asked, "What town are you talking about?" When I said Columbia he replied "You've gotta be kidding me!" When I told him I was serious, he said that at around 1:00am that morning his hounds jumped a deer five miles east of New Bloomfield and headed west. I said it wasn't any wonder the old dog's feet were sore. That's close to thirty miles in a straight line, on frozen ground with a couple of highways and at least two big creeks in between. That old hound definitely had a long hard night.

We got the directions worked out, and I told him that I had to go to town, but I would leave his dog in my stock trailer. When I went out to the truck and drove up to the barn where my trailer was parked the old dog never even moved. I put some straw, a water dish and a pile of dog food in the trailer, and then I shook him 'til he woke up. He did NOT want to get out of that warm truck, but I finally got him drug out and stuffed into the trailer. As soon as I shut the gate on the trailer he sat down and started howling, he didn't want to be left alone. When I got back from town a couple of hours later the dog was gone, but he'd drunk the water, cleaned up the pile of food and wallered out a pretty good bed in the straw pile. I'll bet that tired old hound slept for a week after he got back home.

*   *   *   *   *

When Justin killed his first deer in November 2000, it was right at the end of the day. He and Greg had been hunting on the east side of Bearfield Road, and had walked up to the barn lot to go home. They got in the truck and headed down the lane toward the road, and when they got there they spotted a deer standing west of the road near the red barn, facing north.

Greg stopped, and Justin got out of the truck and eased across the road, then using the gate for a rest he took a shot. The deer leaped straight up, spun around and headed south at a dead run, Justin thought he had missed it completely.

When it reached the pond instead of veering off, it ran straight into the pond until the water was up to its belly, then it stood up on its hind legs, spun around in a circle 2 or 3 times and then slumped into the water, dead. When Greg and Justin dressed the deer they discovered it had done all of that with the bottom half of its heart disintegrated. Justin had made a perfect shot, but adrenaline is amazing stuff.

Hunting has been a tradition in the Easley family for many years. Pappy and Uncle Edward with a nice mess of rabbits, sometime before 1920.

The temperature was just above freezing that afternoon but Greg said, "It's your deer, go get it," so Justin had to wade out in the pond and drag that deer out of the mud and water. He was almost frozen by the time they got back over to Mom's house, but cold or not he was sure 'nuff one proud boy.

Working Construction

When I first went to work for J. Louis Crum as an apprentice plumber, I got paired up with Homer Medley. I didn't have a watch, and usually a couple of times a day I'd ask Homer what time it was.

It didn't matter if it was 9:00am or 4:00pm, Homer would look at his watch and say "It's 2:30, buy a watch you cheap bastard!" I still don't wear a watch, and I 'spect old Homer is looking down and thinking "Buy a watch, you cheap bastard!"

* * * * *

When I worked for J. Louis Crum Corp. while serving my Plumber/Pipefitter Apprenticeship, it was an era when people took pride in their work. I got a really good lesson about that from Morrison Breedlove.

The new MU dorms at college and Ashland Gravel were complete and occupied, but J. Louis had gotten a change order for an extra drinking fountain. We had removed some ceiling tile and Morrison was on a ladder preparing to solder the drain line. He asked me if it was straight and I replied, "Straight enough, when we get those tiles back in no one's going to see it anyhow." Morrison looked at me and said, "Me and Jesus Christ are going to see it, and I don't know about him but I want the damn thing straight."

Me and Morrison Breedlove, early 1980's.

I've thought about that remark a lot of times. It doesn't matter if I'm trimming a door in the house, or building a work bench out of 2" rough-sawed oak, I always think "Well, Morrison and Jesus Christ are going to see this, I'd better get it straight." I've seen a lot of work done that I don't think Morrison or Jesus Christ either one would approve of.

*   *   *   *   *

I worked for quite a few job foreman over the years. Billy Harper, Morrison Breedlove, Wayne Hupp, Vic Jones, Ed Riley, Robert and Jerry McGrath, Dean Vaughn and many others. And of course, Marcia's dad. You didn't have to work for him very long to really make you appreciate the others.

*   *   *   *   *

I worked for Jacob Plumbing Co. for several years. When I was on the Deaf School job in Fulton, Jerry McGrath was foreman, and I worked with his nephew, Patrick.

The porta-pottys were a lot cruder back then than they are now. They were just kind of slapped together out of plywood, with a tin tank. I was setting in the potty one day when Jerry threw a half a concrete block against the door. The door hinges were nailed on instead of screwed, and when that block hit, the nails popped out and the door fell off. Hello, world.

A few days later I saw Jerry go into the potty. There was a coil of rope laying pretty close to where Pat and I were working, so we grabbed the rope, slipped down to the porta-pot, then we each held one end of the rope and circled the potty in opposite directions until we ran out of rope, and then tied it off. We started gently rocking the potty and Jerry started cussing. He questioned our ancestry, sexual preferences, food choices and anything else he could think of. By this time we had the potty tipped back and balanced. I said, "Hang on, Jerry," and we pushed the potty forward. What we didn't realize was that the tank hadn't been pumped out recently, and it was nearly full. When the potty hit the ground, poop chunks and pee water drenched Jerry from the waist down. That was one mad fat man!

Patrick and I decided the other side of the job was the best place for us, so we left Jerry roped in the potty and headed for safer territory. Jerry kept cussing until he finally ran out of breath. When he stopped, an electrician said "Jerry, I don't have a damn thing to do with this, but if you promise not to kill me I'll let you out." He cut the rope and Jerry came out, smelling just like he looked. After he got cleaned up he started looking for Patrick and I, but I'll guaran-damn-tee that we stayed hid for the rest of the day.

*   *   *   *   *

About three weeks later I came down with the flu. My head was stopped up, my nose was running, and every part of my body ached. Of course when you work construction there's no such thing as sick leave, so I just kept dragging in to work. Finally one morning I told Jerry that I felt so bad I was going back to Columbia and try to see a Doctor.

Jerry said, "Let me call my Doctor, I can probably get you in to see him, and you won't have to take off work." Pretty soon Jerry told me that I could go in right then. It was a small office, one doctor and his nurse, who was also the receptionist. I told her who I was and she gave me a big smile and said to come on back. When the doctor came in she told him who I was, then he gave me a big smile and told me to take off my pants and sit on the examining table. I wondered why I needed to take my pants off to get treated for the flu, but I did what I was told.

After I sat down they both stepped in front of me with smiles on their faces. The nurse said, "We understand you have a little problem." I replied, "Yes Mam, I've had the flu for a week, and I feel so bad I can't hardly make it to work." The longer I talked the bigger their smiles got, and by the time I finished they were laughing. I had no idea what was going on. They doctor finally said, "Well, that's not really what we were expecting. Jerry said there was a young man working for him who had a dose of the clap, and he was sending him down for a Penicillin shot." By then I was laughing with them, and I said "Well, that fat son-of-a-bitch owed me one, but I do believe we're even now."

*   *   *   *   *

When I first went to work for Crum - Limbach Corp. on the VA Hospital I got paired up with Charlie Wyand. There were so many guys on that job that there were ass-packets full of foremen, and Bob Victor was our crew foreman for a while.

Charlie and I were working off of 16' stepladders, running copper waterlines. It was around 15 degrees, with a pretty good breeze, and there weren't any walls up, so it was pretty uncomfortable.

Bob came out around 11:30 to check on us. He remarked that it was pretty rough working conditions. Charlie said, "If you can drag your sorry ass out here to check on us, we can damn sure work in it." Bob said, "Kiss my ass," and that was the last we saw of him all day.

*   *   *   *   *

When Hathman Construction Co. built the Lewis and Clark dorms back in the late 1960s, Fuzz Hazell and Ed Carter were moving a crane one morning when the house-lock malfunctioned, the boom swung around and the crane laid over on its side, with the boom extended across Providence Road.

Bo Shely was working for Shorty Hathman at the time. He was as pure black as anyone you'll ever meet. Bo had just stepped out of a porta-potty when he saw the crane starting to tip. He ran out of the way, then stopped and watched the crash. When it was all over the boom had missed the porta-pot by less than 10 feet. Bo looked the situation over, then said "Goddamn, boys, if I'd still been in that crapper when that boom hit I'd have come out of there high yeller."

Not a very politically correct remark if someone else had made it, but since Bo said it himself it was OK.

*   *   *   *   *

Harry Bishop and I both worked for J. Louis Crum Corp. back in the late 1960s. I don't remember for sure which MU building we were working on, but it was a pretty fair sized remodel job on the west side of College Avenue. Harry was pretty big into karate at that time, and he was always wanting to show someone his moves.

One morning before work Harry was prancing around the shack with a screwdriver. Harry said if you knew karate you were safe anywhere you went because if you had a weapon no one could take it away from you. Forrest Cowden, who had been a Ranger during World War II, walked in while Harry was prancing around. As Forrest walked past, Harry twitched the screwdriver in his direction.

I saw what happened, but I still don't know how it happened. In a flash Forrest took the screwdriver away from Harry and poked the handle into Harry's stomach so hard that it knocked his breath out and sat him on his butt on the floor. Forrest tossed the screwdriver down and said "Harry, I believe you need to work on that just a little more." We didn't hear any more about karate for a long time.

*   *   *   *   *

Dude Clemons didn't want anyone with any authority watching him work. One day J. Louis Crum walked up where Dude was hooking up a window unit. Dude laid his tools down and started visiting with J. Louis. After a few minutes Louie said "Dude, you know you could work while we talk." Dude said, "I was hired to do it, not show you how to do it. I'll talk 'til you leave, then I'll go back to work." Louie shook his head and said, "Damned independent welders!" then walked away.

*   *   *   *   *

Generally when you went to work for a different contractor you would receive a very basic set of tools. B.J. Dukes had worked for J. Louis Crum long enough that he had collected a pretty impressive set of hand tools. I worked with Dukes for a while on the Math Science Building at MU, where Wayne Hupp was foreman. Dukes was leaving for a weeks' vacation and the afternoon before he left he told me "I don't want no one messing with my tools while I'm gone so I'm going to padlock my handbox, you can borrow tools for a week."

That worked for a couple of days, but one afternoon I needed some tool, and I asked Hupp if he could get me one. He said I should have one, and I replied there were probably 2 or 3 in B.J.'s box, but he locked it before he left. Wayne was pissed. He said, "That son-of-a-bitch, those aren't his tools. He's going to be mad about this, so I'll do it myself and he can be mad at me." Wayne got a cutting torch, but he didn't just cut the lock off Dukes' box, he cut the handles off, then he opened the lids and cut them off.

The morning Dukes got back, when we headed towards the building Hupp wandered along behind. Dukes unlocked the gang box, then hollered "What the damn hell happened?" Hupp stepped up and said, "I cut the damn lids off the damn toolbox so Alan could use the damn tools, do you have a damn problem with that?" Dukes started mouthing and Wayne said, "If you don't like it I'll send the whole damn box back to the shop, and you can start collecting tools from scratch." Dukes didn't like that idea, so he just shut up. He was pretty grumpy for a few days but he eventually got over it.

*   *   *   *   *

When the MU dorms at College Avenue and Rollins were under construction, Dukes walked into the shack one morning and stopped just inside the door. I thought he had been in a car wreck. His whole face was bruised, his eyes were almost swollen shut, and his jaws were swollen so bad you couldn't see his neck. He said, "I had a goddamn fight, I won, and I don't want to hear a bunch of crap about it." I can't imagine what the loser must have looked like.

It seems that Dukes and Estill Hudson (Lying Estill, not good Estill) had a fight at Chub's Club the night before. They used fists, feet, beer bottles and chairs and finally went through the glass entry door and wound up grinding each other's faces into the gravel parking lot. Dukes was the last one who was able to get up without help, so he claimed he won.

If a fight like that happened now, every cop car in the City of Columbia would be there, Dukes and Estill would get tazed, have guns pointed at them, be handcuffed and then get their asses hauled to jail. Back then, the cops weren't even notified. Everyone just tried to stay out of the way, and when it was all over, Chub Armstrong told them "When you sorry bastards feel a little better, get your worthless asses back out here, 'cause you owe me some damages." I don't know how much it cost them, but Dukes and Estill paid the damages and the Police never even knew that the fight had taken place. Life was a lot simpler back then.

*   *   *   *   *

Jim Potter and I worked together for J. Louis Crum on the Biggs Building addition (Criminal Insane Building) at Fulton. There was an electrician on the job who we messed with all the time, just because he was so damned easy. He didn't understand bullshit and anything and everything that we did made him mad.

Jim and I were working in a utility tunnel that ran between two buildings. We were running copper water lines, 4" cold, 2" hot and a 1" hot water return line. At one set of hangers the electrician had left his coat laying. Jim and I looked at each other and had the same idea. I started to run a length of 2" copper through the coat sleeves, but Jim said since we'd eventually have to retrieve the coat we might as well use 1" pipe because it would be easier to repair. We slipped a length of 1" copper through the coat sleeves, and continued running pipe.

It was several days before the temperature dropped and the electrician went looking for his coat. Jim and I were setting sleeves on the 2nd floor deck when we suddenly heard "You sorry, no-good bastards!" He was coming across the deck as fast as he could stumble over the re-rods, and he was pissed! He said, "I'm going back down to that damn tunnel in 5 minutes, and if I can't pick my coat up and walk away with it, I'm going to chop that son-of-a-bitch off that goddamn water line with an axe." I said, "What happened, dumbass, did you leave your coat laying in the wrong place?" As he walked off he said, "You common assholes."

Jim and I got our torch, solder, copper cutters, etc., and headed for the tunnel. Unfortunately, Wilkie (Marcia's dad) walked up just as Jim finished cutting the line and I was starting to slip the coat off. He stood there watching us, then he rolled his cigar from one side of his mouth to the other and asked, "What the hell's going on?" I said, "Oh, some dumb assed electrician got his coat stuck on our pipe and we had to get it off for him." Wilkie rolled that cigar back where it started from, then said "Damn kids," and walked off.

*　　*　　*　　*　　*

On the same job, Jim and I were running soil pipe on the ground floor. Our location for a floor drain was 18" from the outside wall. We cut our pipe and laid it in the ditch, then took a check measurement before making the joint. I said, "Hell Jim, we're a foot to short," so we proceeded to pull the pipe out, cut a foot off of it, and then measured again. I said, "Hell Jim, we're 2' short now."

J. Louis Crum had walked up and watched this whole operation. After we took the second check measurement he said "Goddamn, I can't believe that I'm actually paying you boys," and then he turned and walked away.

*   *   *   *   *

I was talking to Andy Rule during Patrick McGrath's visitation at the Millersburg Lions Club, when he asked me if I remembered the time Jim Potter and I caught up with Wilkie on our way home from work. I'd forgotten all about it, but it came back to me real quick.

It never really mattered if I was working with Potter, Charlie Weyand, Patrick, Andy, Charlie Lee or someone else, back in those days working construction was fun, and we always had something stirred up.

Potter and I were working for J. Louis Crum at the Biggs Building in Fulton and Wilkie (Marcia's dad) was Foreman. One afternoon around 3:00 he told us that he needed to talk to J. Louis, so he was heading back to Columbia. That sounded good to us, so as soon as he climbed in his pickup we started putting up our tools. He hadn't much more than pulled onto the street before we were heading towards the parking area.

We'd forgotten how slow Wilkie drove, and when we topped the last hill before we got into Fulton there he was puttering down the road. I had to get on the brakes pretty hard to keep from rear-ending him.

*   *   *   *   *

That wasn't the last time that Potter "cut it a little green" at quitting time, either. When we were working at the VA Hospital in Columbia he slipped out to his car one afternoon around 4:00, and headed out the back side of the parking lot. There was quite a bit of traffic on the street, and while he was setting there waiting to pull out, J. Louis Crum pulled in. Jim said, "What the hell, I couldn't hide, so I just waved at him as he went by."

*   *   *   *   *

Potter was sharp as hell, and he was good with the tools, but no one ever accused him of setting any speed records.

Charlie Lee told me that Ernie Gholson walked up to him on the job one afternoon and asked to borrow a piece of soapstone. He said, "Charlie, I'm going to draw a circle around that damn Potter, so I can tell if he moves between now and quitting time."

*   *   *   *   *

Charlie Lee and I spent one cold winter working on a new cell block at the Moberly Prison. There was a plumber from somewhere in Kansas working there also. Norm was functional, but he damn sure wasn't overqualified. One day Charlie noticed Norm standing on a step ladder with his 6' rule folded out, and stretching his arm out at an angle with the rule sagging.

Charlie asked him what he was doing, and he replied he had to make a 45-degree offset and he was trying to get a measurement. I said, "Why don't you use the formula? It's a hell of a lot easier than that." He looked at me and asked, "What formula?" I told him to get off the ladder and I'd show him. There was a 2' square concrete column near where we were working so I grabbed a piece of chalk out of my tool box and walked over to the column.

I said, "Norm, how long is the offset?" He said 29," so I reached as high as I could reach, wrote 29.0," then started writing every algebra equation I could remember from high school, some long division, square root of my birthday, Pi x anything I could think of and I drew a few squares and triangles for good measure. Somewhere in the middle of the column I took 29" x 1.41, came up with 40.89" and just kept writing. by the time I finished I was on my knees, writing almost at floor level. The last line had about a dozen numbers, ending in 40.89. I underlined it and said "There you go, Norm. Don't forget to take off for your fittings, then cut it a shy 41," center to center, and it'll work."

It was about lunch time by then, so Charlie and I headed to the shack to eat. We thought Norm was behind us, but when we got there he was nowhere in sight. We ate lunch, and when we got back to the building Norm had worked through lunch and had the offset installed. He was sitting on top of the stepladder, staring at what he had done. When he saw us he said, "That son-of-a-bitch fit, but I still don't know how you did it." I said, "I just used the formula, Norm, there's nothing to it." We never did tell poor old Norm how we did it.

*   *   *   *   *

A few days after that, Charlie and I and John Brown and Norm were making water and sewer connections to one of the guard towers. It was so muddy we couldn't hardly walk, there was water standing in the ditches, and it was starting to rain. Normally we would have gone to the dry, but we wanted to finish and be done with that slop-hole before it came another big rain.

Charlie and I had just finished our water tie in, and John and Norm had one more poured joint to make. They had rigged a little plywood roof over the lead pot, in an attempt to keep the rain out of that hot lead. Charlie and I were heading to the guard tower with our tools when we heard John call for hot lead. We put our tools up, and when we came out John was still hollering for Norm to bring him some lead. We didn't see Norm so we took John a ladle of lead. He got that last joint poured and caulked, and tossed his tools up out of the ditch. We helped John get his tools inside, then we started looking for Norm.

By this time it was raining pretty hard, and we finally found Norm sitting in his truck with the heater on, listening to the radio and running the wind shield wipers so that he could see what was going on. John almost lost it, he said "I'm gonna kill that dumb, lazy bastard, I'll stomp his worthless ass into the bottom of that ditch." I 'spect he'd have tried if Charlie and I hadn't kept him off.

Not long after that the foreman decided that sitting on the bench in a union hall in Kansas was probably a better place for Norm to spend his time than working on the Moberly Prison. I don't think that John was sorry to see him go.

*   *   *   *   *

Jim Potter and I worked together on the Math Science Building for several months. There was a long 2 x 12 shelf in the shack where everyone sat their lunch boxes. Someone nailed Jim's box to the shelf one Monday afternoon with double headed forming nails. When Jim started to pick it up at quitting time he realized there was a problem. He opened the box, saw the problem, got a claw hammer and pulled the nails, and then went home.

The exact same thing happened on Tuesday, Wednesday, and Thursday. On Friday Jim was anxious to get the hell out of there and start the weekend. He grabbed his lunch box as he went by and jerked the handle off the box. Jim said, "Oh bullshit," then pulled the nails and left with his lunch box under his arm. On Monday J. Louis Crum paid Jim and I to make a replacement handle out of 1/2" copper pipe and attach it to Jim's lunch box.

*   *   *   *   *

Most of the people who worked in the office for Crum Corp. were pretty decent to get along with, but J. Louis hired one pompous assed engineer who thought he was just damn near too good to have to come on the job with all those crude construction workers.

Jim Potter and I were coming out of the shack at the Math Science Building one afternoon just as Mr. Big was coming in. It was like we didn't exist. After he went in the shack I said "Jim, I just can't stand that big feeling piece of shit." Jim said he couldn't either. The guy had parked his Chrysler in front of the shack, and as we walked past the car Jim glanced in and said that the keys were in it. I told him to get the car and I would find a good place for it. On the far side of the jobsite was a large pile of black dirt that had been skimmed off and piled up months before. Horse weeds were 10' tall on the pile. I motioned to Jim and he took the car around behind the pile and parked it.

We were working on the second floor, so we went on back to where we were working and stood around waiting for that asshole to come out of the shack. When he finally walked out he looked around, then started waving his arms and hollering. We couldn't hear what he was saying, but before long Wayne Hupp came out of the shack. The guy kept hollering, and we could tell Wayne was trying to calm him down. Finally a carpenter walked by and Wayne said something to him. He kinda shrugged his shoulders and pointed towards the dirt pile.

Mr. Pompous ass was pissed! As he went stomping across the jobsite toward his car, Wayne was standing there grinning like a dog eating shit, apparently he didn't like the guy, either. All in all, it was definitely worth our effort.

*   *   *   *   *

Karl DeMarce and me, January 1972. The sign on my hard-hat says "Jacob Plbg. and Htg."

Charlie Weyand and I worked together for about a year on the Ash Street pump station for Jacob Plumbing and Heating. Robert McGrath was the job foreman and anyone who couldn't work for Robert didn't deserve to have a job.

Charlie was recently divorced and he was partying pretty hard every night. One evening Bill Blackwell and I had some big project going on, and I drank a little (whole bunch) too much beer while we were taking care of our chore. I flat felt like hell the next morning, and when I pulled into the parking lot at the job I thought "Well, I've carried Charlie quite a bit lately, I believe he can carry me today." Before I got out of my truck Charlie pulled in and parked next to me. When he started to get out of his car his legs buckled and he fell flat on his face. I had to help him get up. We decided to bypass the job shack and go straight to where we were working.

We were installing big pumps in a sub-basement, the stairs weren't built yet, and the only way to get there was down a 25' extension ladder. I told Charlie he needed to go down first because I didn't want his drunken ass to fall on top of me. We made it safely down the ladder, but neither of us was in any mood to work. Charlie found some sacks, and a coat someone had forgotten and made himself a bed on the concrete floor. I found an old tarp in the corner and wadded it up and made myself a pretty good nest.

Around 9:00 I heard a racket and saw Robert coming down the ladder. Our tool box was still locked and Robert wasn't no dummy so I didn't see much reason to jump up. When he got to the basement he found me sitting on that wadded-up tarp, reading a gun magazine. Robert looked at me and kinda smiled and then walked over and nudged Charlie in the ribs 2 or 3 times with the toe of his cowboy boot. Charlie grunted and rolled over, but didn't wake up. Robert looked at me and shook his head, smiled again and said, "Today's yours, but by God tomorrow is MINE, and don't you forget it." He went back up the ladder and that was the last time I saw him 'til the next morning.

Charlie and I pretty much spent the day napping and when we weren't napping we were talking. We never did unlock the tool box. On our way to the parking lot that afternoon I told Charlie it would probably be a good night not to drink any beer because we owed Robert a good one. Charlie stayed straight and we gave Robert a hell of a good days work the next day. Someone like Robert always got more out of their crew in the long run, than some asshole who was always yelling and trying to crack the whip.

*   *   *   *   *

When I worked at the trade there were a lot of family groups in Local 317. Fathers and sons, uncles and nephews, brothers, cousins, in-laws, outlaws, and what have you.

I never tried to count them all, but there were a bunch of McGraths', several Gholsons', several Vaughns', some Rileys', Lees', and Bachs', Jack, Dude, and Danny Clemons, and of course everyone remembers the Breedlove Brothers.

Morrison Breedlove was as fine a gentleman as I ever met, he was easy to work for and fun to work with. Nim was fun to work with too, the only problem I ever had working with Nim was that my ribs were always sore from laughing so hard. And then there was Hurley; I don't know what the hell happened there. Hurley always looked like he had just bit into a green persimmon, and most of the time he acted about how he looked. Oh well, I reckon 2 out of 3 ain't bad.

*   *   *   *   *

Once when I was working for Jacob Plbg., Floyd Andrews and I were paired up on a little job over at Fulton. We were the only two on the job, and I guess that wasn't enough to rate a power hack-saw. Anyhow, one afternoon I was cutting hanger rods by hand when Floyd walked up. I had been clamping three rods at a time in the pipe vise and then cutting them. Floyd watched while I sawed three rods, then he said, "That'll take forever, I'll show you how to cut hanger rods." He laid a length of all-thread on the vise and then grabbed the cutting torch. I said, "Oh hell, Floyd, this is going to work simply wonderful."

After he had cut a dozen or so he picked one up and tried to start a nut on it. He tried both ends with no luck, then tried a couple more with the same results. As he started to walk away he looked back and said, "You'll need to file those a little bit so the nuts will start." I said "Andy, you file the son-of-a-bitches, you screwed them up!" He glared at me, then kicked all of his rods under the work-bench and stomped off. I don't know what he did next, but I got my hack-saw and went back to cutting hanger rods by hand.

Good Old Dogs

We've had lots of good old dogs over the years. Hell, you can't live 70 some years without having several good ones, and a few really good ones.

The first dog I remember was spot. She was born to be a registered Rat Terrier, but she got about three times as big as she should have, and was born with a stub tail. She was basically worthless, but she loved her people.

Alan and Spot, around 1945

We got her when she was just a pup, but we'd never let her come in the house until one really cold morning after she had gotten pretty old. She was sitting outside the kitchen door with her teeth chattering, so Mom felt sorry for her and invited her in the house. Spot wasn't real sure about that, but she finally came in and looked around real cautiously. Pretty soon she walked over to the woodstove and went between it and the wall. She laid down, let out a big sigh, and went to sleep.

Old Spot lived another two or three years, and she spent most of that time behind the stove, both winter and summer. She soon figured out that if her teeth were chattering she could come in the house, so it could be a hundred degrees outside and if someone went to the door she would look at them and chatter her teeth. We always thought old Spot was kind of dumb, but maybe she was smarter than we gave her credit for.

*   *   *   *   *

Other dogs we had when I was growing up were Pudge, Wag and Pancake. Pudge was old Spot's pup. The other two just showed up. Pudge was Pappy's all-time favorite dog. He got run over by a concrete truck on my 12th birthday.

Pancake showed up at the back door one Sunday morning, about starved. The only thing I could find to feed her were some cold pancakes left over from breakfast. She snarfed them down and decided she'd found a home. She was a pretty good little dog.

*   *   *   *   *

Back when the kids were still pretty small and I was working construction, as I headed towards my truck one morning to go to work I noticed a half-starved little yellow mutt-dog peeking around the corner of the house. I said, "Hey, dog, what're you doing?" When I spoke, she ran like I'd shot at her. I went back in the house and got some table scraps and dumped them in a pile, then I went on to work. The scraps were gone when I got home, but I didn't see the dog.

The next two mornings were the same. She would peek around the corner, and I would say, "Hey, Dog," and dump a pile of scraps. Marcia and the boys started asking me about "Hey Dog" every morning. Along about the fourth morning, when I dumped her food, I backed way up and just stood there talking trash to her. She finally slipped up to the pile and grabbed a mouthful, then ran off to eat it. For the next several days, I stood a little closer to the pile each day. Finally she would eat with me standing there. It was several more days before she would take food out of my hand.

The first time I laid my hand on her while she was eating, she just hunkered down and looked at me like she expected to get a beating. For several days we followed the same routine, and she always looked at me like she couldn't understand why I didn't go ahead and beat her. She finally decided that I wasn't going to hit her, and she started to enjoy the petting.

It took several more days for her to decide that the boys weren't going to hurt her, but after that she started spending a lot of time with them. Hey Dog wouldn't get close to Marcia for quite a while, because she swept the garage and front porch every morning and Hey Dog thought that brooms were made to beat dogs with. She finally accepted the fact that Marcia wasn't going to hit her, and after that they were buddies, but she never did get over her fear of brooms.

Hey Dog

She was a four people dog for a long time, but after two or three years, she finally decided that Pappy and Mom were okay, and when they came visiting she would stay around and let them pet her. If anyone else came by, she just disappeared. We never noticed her leave, but we wouldn't see her again 'til after our company was gone.

Hey Dog wouldn't live 24 hours on this road today, but back then there was very little traffic and everyone knew to watch out for "Easley's old mutt." She loved to lay in the middle of the road and sleep, because the gravel was warm. She got pretty deaf in her old age, and when she was sleeping in the road and a car came along she just laid there until the vibration woke her up, then she would raise her head and look around to see what was happening, then lay back down. Everyone that came down the road would almost stop, then pull to the edge of the road as they went around her. She didn't mind people driving on her bed but she wasn't about to move for them.

Hey Dog was fairly old when she showed up here, but she lived another five or six years, and pretty much enjoyed her old age.

*   *   *   *   *

The first dog that Marcia and I got for the boys was a black, short-haired border collie that came from Lloyd Haley. For some reason, the dog got named "Fish Hook." That was the groundhog hatingest dog I ever saw in my life. When he was about 2/3 grown he jumped on a young ground hog one afternoon, and it bit through his lower lip and held on. We heard him howling, and when we went outside to see what was going on he was spinning in circles so fast that most of the time the groundhog was in the air, but occasionally it would hit the ground and bounce. Fish Hook's lip kept stretching out longer and longer until it finally ripped out, releasing the groundhog. It hit the ground running and Fish Hook jumped it and didn't turn it loose for at least 45 minutes. When he finally quit chewing there wasn't a piece left bigger than a half-dollar. Fish Hook killed lots of groundhogs over the years, and he always shredded them after he killed them.

He got where he roamed a lot, and one day he just disappeared for good. Several years after that I was sitting on Harold Johnson's porch one morning, when the conversation finally worked its way around to dogs. Harold said, "You know, I've never told a soul about this, but several years ago, there was a real pretty black dog that got to coming by here 2 or 3 times a week and he'd always run my bird dogs away from their food dish and clean it out."

"One day, I saw him eating and I thought to myself, old dog, I'm going to burn you a little bit and maybe you'll stop coming by here. I got my shotgun and some #7 ½ shells, and took a shot at him. I expected him to howl and run, but when I shot he dropped to his stomach and never moved again. I ran down there and there was a little spec of blood in one eye. A pellet had hit him in the eye and gone into his brain. I really hated that, I didn't have any intention of killing him. I took his collar off and threw it into the pond, and drug the dog across the road onto Oscar Elley's and covered him up with brush. I never did find out who he belonged to."

I didn't tell Harold that the old dog was mine, he felt plenty bad enough about what had happened without knowing it was my dog.

*   *   *   *   *

When the boys were little, C.J. Tekotte had a litter of beagle pups for sale. One morning Marcia and I took the boys to Tekotte's to pick out a pup.

They were under the back porch, and when Jay called them the first one that came out was a gawky, awkward, loose-hided pup with one brown eye and one blue eye and feet that were way too big for his body. Marcia looked at him and said, "That's the ugliest pup I've ever seen in my whole life!" I replied, "Yeah, he sure is, and he's mine, you all can pick out another one." The boys picked out a nice, normal looking pup, and we headed home with the pair. The boys named their pup C.J. after Tekotte, and the goofy looking one wound up being called Bruno.

Marcia thought Bruno was dumb, but I told her that he was just cautious and kind of slow moving. If C.J. saw something he found interesting Bruno would hang back at least 50 feet, 'til C.J. checked it out and made sure it was safe. When the boys would ride their bikes to Blackwell's or Gene Brown's, the dogs would follow them. C.J. would get there about the same time they did, but sometimes on their way home they would meet Bruno, he hadn't even gotten there yet.

Bruno and C.J.

There was a worthless bastard who lived north of Brown's for a while who was stealing dogs and selling them to an experimental lab in Jefferson City. The Sheriff's Department was watching him, but they couldn't ever catch him doing it. C.J. and Bruno disappeared one day and we never saw them again. I always figured that no-good, rotten, son-of-a-bitch stole our beagles and sold them to that lab. He was damn lucky I never found out for sure!

*   *   *   *   *

Pappy died in February 1982. Just a couple of days before he went to the hospital I became the proud owner of a couple of Black and Tan/Walker cross coon hound pups, one male and one female. I hadn't named them yet, and somehow they wound up being Ben and Leon, after two old men in the hospital room next to Pappy. Leon was the female but she didn't mind that she had a boy's name.

Leon pretty much left vehicles alone, but Ben always raced the school bus. He would run 'til he passed it, then cut across the road in front of it and run down the other side for a while. One morning he timed it wrong, and the bus got him. The way

Ol' Leon

Leon howled, you would have thought she was the one who had been run over.

I buried Ben by the machine shed, and every morning for the next week Leon would wake us up, howling. When she got up she would go sit in the middle of the road, where Ben was killed, and howl for 15 or 20 minutes. Then she would lay by Ben's grave and whine for another 15 or 20 minutes before she finally came to the house for breakfast. She kept this up off and on for a month before she finally got over losing Ben.

After Ben got killed, Leon turned into a truck hound, and she went with me all day, every day, it didn't matter what I was doing. One fall, she scared a deer just as some no-good, sorry-assed son-of-a-bitch was getting ready to shoot it, so the rotten bastard shot her instead. Doc Kinkead was a neighbor back then, and he donated lots of time, money and expertise over the next four months, and he saved my old hound. Thanks, Doc.

*   *   *   *   *

Reese Reeder, 1990

This might be a machinery story, or it might be a dog story, but it's got to go somewhere so I'm calling it a dog story and putting it here.

One summer about a week before wheat harvest time, Reese Reeder from Modern Farm Equipment Co. was at the farm, getting my combine ready to go. The combine was parked in the red barn west of our house. When the combine was in the barn there was only about 3 inches of clearance between the machine and the trusses, so when Reese was on top of the combine, he had to be really careful that he didn't hit his head.

I had been hand-feeding some calves that winter and spring, and there were two big piles of empty feed sacks behind the combine. I don't know why old Leon wasn't with me that day, but instead she was spending her time up at the barn with Reese.

Reese had the sliding doors open on both ends of the barn, so he could get a breeze. He was on his knees on top of the combine when Leon jumped a rabbit in the barn lot. It ran in the north door and out the south door into the field. Leon entered the barn behind it at full speed and decided she could go through the pile of sacks easier than she could go around it. When she hit that pile of dry paper sacks it made a hell of a racket, and it startled Reese so bad he straightened up to see what was going on. When he stood up, he hit his head on the barn roof so hard it almost knocked him out. Reese told me, "Alan, I like that worthless old hound, but I wish you'd teach her to go around those sacks, I don't think my head could stand to do that again!"

*   *   *   *   *

One afternoon I was cutting beans east of the house, on the place that belongs to Jan Hayes now.

Rabbits were thick that year, and Old Leon was having a ball chasing them. She was fast enough in her prime that she could outrun one occasionally and catch it. Once I looked out in front of the combine a little ways and saw a rabbit headed toward me at full speed, with Leon about six feet behind it with her nose to the ground. That rabbit was running for its life, Leon was running for her supper, and neither one of them was paying any attention to where that was taking them. I stopped and raised the header, and the rabbit and Leon both ran under the header and out the back. I honest to God believe that if I hadn't raised the header that day, they both would have run right into it and gone through the combine.

*   *   *   *   *

Skeeter was Marcia's dog, but he pretty much grabbed ahold of me too. A few years after Leon died Marcia told me that she had seen a beautiful little dog at the shelter, and she wanted me to go with her to look at it.

When we got there she signed him out, and an attendant brought him to us. Marcia said, "Hon, isn't he the most beautiful little thing you ever saw in your life?" Un-huh! He was half-starved, boney, and he had

Skeeter

so many fleas that half of his hair was scratched out

leaving big bald scabby spots, and what hair he did have was snaggled and knotted so bad that it would never get un-tangled. I said, "Yeah, Babe, he's just amazingly beautiful." She said, "I knew you'd like him, here, take the leash and walk him for a while and I'll go sign the papers."

She sure saw something that first day that I didn't see, but it was there. We had him for almost seven years before he died, and he pretty much made himself one of the family. And he was actually a really pretty little dog, after he gained some weight and grew all of his hair back.

*   *   *   *   *

Old Cloe is Stephen's dog, and when he started living with us going on seven years ago, Cloe came with him. She was going to live in a doghouse on the patio, then she was going to live in the basement, then Marcia decided it would be okay if she came upstairs as long as she stayed in the hallway.

Marcia spent a lot of time in her sewing room, so before long Cloe started slipping into the sewing room so that she could get a little petting. She gained access to the dining room next, because she needed to lay in front of the Buck stove when it was cold. Next she got the kitchen, because that's where the food is and she needed a little snack occasionally.

The pink carpet in the family room stayed off limits for quite a while, but Cloe finally started nudging her way an inch or two farther into the room every day, until finally Marcia walked in the room one afternoon and Cloe was on the far side of the room, laying in front of the stove. My Baby walked over and gave Cloe a belly rub with her foot, then said "Cloe, Cloe, Cloe, you're a mess, what am I going to do with you?" Cloe has had the whole house ever since.

After Marcia died Cloe spent the next three weeks, wandering from room to room, looking for her. Cloe would check the bedroom, then the sewing room, then she would walk into the kitchen and stand in front of the sink looking around. Her last stop was always the family room, where she would stand for ten or fifteen minutes and whine while she looked at the empty couch. She doesn't mind me leaving her at home if it's warm enough she can stay outside, but she doesn't want to be alone in the house, so she's pretty much turned into a truck hound.

Cloe

Old Cloe will be my last dog. When Pappy was up in his 70's, he said he'd never have another dog because it hurt too bad to bury them. I know what he meant. After Cloe is gone if I want to pet a dog, I'll just go to the Greg and Jamie's for a while, but I've buried enough dogs over the years, and I don't want to have to do it anymore.

*   *   *   *   *

When I was a kid, Cavcey's had a long-haired red shepherd dog named Trooper. He was pretty much John and Kenny's dog, but he loved company.

Hale and Gladys both worked, and Kenny, John and Carol were in school, so every day after the school bus left Trooper would come to our house. It didn't make any difference what Pappy was doing, the old dog would spend the day with him 'til about time for the school bus. Pappy said it didn't matter where he was on the farm, at a certain time every day Trooper would stop, look in the direction of home and then head that way. He always got there before the bus did, and would be waiting at the end of the driveway when the kids got off.

Trooper was one of the friendliest dogs you'd ever run across, he loved everybody. I don't remember why he started doing it, but he liked to grin at people. If you pointed your finger at him he would curl his lips back 'til all of his teeth were showing, and then shake his head at you.

Hale ordered some concrete one Saturday, and when the truck pulled in, the driver got out to see where he was going to unload. When Trooper came running up to greet him the guy held out his hand to fend off what he thought was a dog attack. Trooper saw that hand pointing at him and grinned. Hale said that driver didn't waste time opening the truck door, he just dived from the ground up, went through the window and refused to get back out 'til Hale locked up "That damn vicious dog!" He told me it was all he could do to keep from laughing out loud.

Left: Pappy and a litter of pups, mid 1930's

Below: Stephen with   pulling tractors   and "Crazy Abby"

Working at Boonville

I worked for MFA in Boonville for 14 1/2 years. When I first started "Axle Bob" Carmichal worked part time, driving a tender truck during fertilizer season, and a nurse truck during spray season. Bob worked 'til he was well up in his 70s and I always loved to mess with him. When I started spreading fertilizer for MFA they were running a pretty rinky-dink operation, they just had one little single axle tender truck, and Bob was supposed to take that one truck and tender me, Bert Hilden, and any buggies that were running at the time. It kept Bob busy!

That was before we had cell phones, so we stayed in touch the best we could with some junky-assed two-way radios. There was a base unit at the office, one at the fertilizer plant, and a mobile unit in each truck. We could usually hear some loud-mouthed old woman who dispatched the OATS bus in Columbia a lot better than we could hear each other.

When Bob was bringing me a load of fertilizer I would wait 'til I saw him coming down the road, then I'd get on the radio and say "What's taking so long, Bob, where are you at? I'm sitting here waiting on you." He'd reply "Dammit, Baby, pull your head out and look, I'm turning in the gate." When he'd get there he'd tell me, "Dammit, Baby, Clarence is setting on his lazy ass in the Office listening to you, and he thinks you're wasting time 'cause I'm not here. You're going to get me fired, I wish you'd quit that crap."

The next load we'd do the same thing all over again. I don't think Bob ever did figure out that I was just messing with him.

*   *   *   *   *

Bob had a little grey poodle that always rode with him in his van. That was pretty much a one-man dog, but he would let me pet him on the head a little bit, until I started talking to him. I'd say, "Damn, you're just about the right size to make good fish bait. I think I'll hook your curly little ass on a trotline and catch me a big old catfish."

That little dog would look at me, then turn and walk across Bob's lap and get between Bob and the van door, and then duck his head down so I couldn't see him. He didn't know what I was talking about, but whatever it was he was sure he didn't want any part of it.

*   *   *   *   *

One evening around 7:00 Mike Ashley sent me to some rat hole of a farm east of New Franklin, to spray some corn. My directions were "Go past the barn, through a gate, then follow the road down a long hill, and the field is on the other side of the creek." As usual, the directions sucked. They didn't mention that I should unload at the barn and drive the sprayer to the field because there was no way in hell to take a truck and trailer down that hill. After you started down there was no way in hell to turn around or back up the hill either, so I kept going 'til the truck bumper and trailer tongue dug into the ground while I was crossing a ditch, effectively stopping forward progress.

I called the office on my half-assed radio, but they'd all gone home for the day. I tried Axle Bob's mobile, but he was gone for the day too. I knew the other spray trucks were still out somewhere, so I called the mobile units of Steve Crowley, Ronnie Anderson, and Jamie Humphrey, and just for good measure I added "Or anyone listening who gives a shit!" That got results. Steve immediately answered "Alan, I don't give a shit." Ronnie and Jamie had the same response. I said, "Dammit, I'm stuck and I need a pull," but they were all north of Blackwater, at least 20 miles from where I was setting. Jamie went to a phone and called Axle Bob at home and he came after me in a ton truck. He said, "Baby, we're going home, we'll worry about that stuck piece of junk in the morning."

The next morning I unloaded the sprayer and Bob pulled the truck and trailer out and drug my ass backwards up that hill. I mixed up a 500-gallon batch of Atrazine and headed down the hill, and proceeded to drag the drain valve off the bottom of the sprayer while crossing that same damn ditch. When I got to the field and stopped to open the gate I noticed the tank was empty. I guaran-damn-tee that there weren't any weeds growing on that road for a couple of years.

I still hate that damn sorry-assed excuse for a farm!

*   *   *   *   *

The first summer that I ran the sprayer I didn't know anyone around Boonville, and I sure didn't know where anyone's farm was located. However, Clarence and Mike were real good about giving me a stack of spray orders that would keep me busy 'til dark, then around 5:30 they'd go home, and everything had better work because no one would be around to answer a call on the radio.

One afternoon I wound up out in the Lone Elm area just before dark. As I was leaving the field I buried the old truck. I called the office and the other mobile units, but I was the only one still out. I didn't know anyone in the area, so I decided I'd just unload the sprayer and drive it back to Boonville. A couple of miles down the road I spotted an old fella out in his yard. I'd never met him, but it turned out he was Ronnie Anderson's Grandpaw. I told him I was stuck, and asked him if he could give me a ride to Boonville. He said no problem, so I parked the Wilmar and got in the car with him.

He was probably over 80 years old, but when he pulled on the road he stuck his foot to the floor and we headed towards Boonville. You wouldn't believe a little old car could run so fast. He drove with one hand, and looked at me instead of the road about half the time while he talked. If he caught up with another car he just whipped out and passed them.

About halfway to town I glanced up and silently said "Lord, if you'll get me back to Boonville in one piece, I swear that the next time I get stuck I'll just walk back. Thank you, and AMEN." He must have heard me, cause we made it to town in one piece, but damn that was one wild ride!

*   *   *   *   *

At the east end of the chemical building at New Franklin there was a big pothole in the driveway. All it needed was 2 or 3 loader buckets of gravel, but MFA didn't believe in pissing money away on gravel, so the hole just kept on getting bigger. When you pulled out with a load you could drive real slow and go through the hole, or you could swing wide and miss it, but this put you in the wrong lane when you pulled onto the street.

Mike Anderson swung wide one day and headed south in the wrong lane. A young lady speeding up the street in the other direction hit him head-on. Little Mikey told the New Franklin cops "The dumb bitch should have seen me, I was on her side of the street." For some reason the Police weren't real impressed with that remark.

Little Mikey found a hole, May 2000

*　　*　　*　　*　　*

Bob Biesemeyer's Mother's farm was a little bit swampy when conditions were good, and in a wet year it was worse than that. I pulled in one day with the Wilmar to spray corn for Bob. With Bob you always did it his way, whether that was the best way or not. He had me start on the far side of the field, next to a slough. The river was rising pretty fast, and by the time I finished the field twelve or fifteen quarter mile long rows were completely under water.

I told Bob I sure was glad he had me start on the low side, because I wouldn't have got to spray near as many acres if I had started on the high side. Since his corn was going under water, Bob didn't really see the humor in that remark, but that's okay, he always took himself pretty damn serious and he needed to be poked a little bit occasionally anyhow.

*　　*　　*　　*　　*

I don't know why I always got accused of everything, but anytime Jack Pipes would come home and find his driveway, pond dam and the gravel area in front of his machine shed covered with blobs of pink foam, he always thought I'd done it. I wonder why?

*   *   *   *   *

Someone un-hooked from a funky-assed old house trailer on Jack Pipes' bottom farm one afternoon. They were supposed to hook back up and move it almost immediately, but it sat there for a long time. Someone placed a sign in front of the trailer one night, "Opening Soon, Jack's Place, Beer, Food, XXX Girls!". Jack took a lot of crap about his "Beer, Food, and XXX Girls." Unfortunately the old trailer burned before "Jack's Place" was able to open, but that's probably just as well. I don't 'spect Pam would have let Jack run a girly-house for very long, anyhow.

*   *   *   *   *

If you see Jack Pipes, ask him about the elephants and the bowl of Jell-O in his bean field.

*   *   *   *   *

After MFA sold their old fertilizer plant to Fuqua Homes they leased an old funky-assed facility from Pete Davis, temporarily. (Temporarily, as in 10 or 12 years.)

The facility had no office (they set up a job-site trailer), no running water, (we bought bottled water from Snoddy's store for drinking and hauled water from Boonville in jugs and dumped it into a tank for wash water. Of course with no running water there were no sanitary facilities, so they rented a chemical porta-potty.

When the porta-potty people would pump out the tank they would always put about a foot of chemically treated water in the tank to control odor. The water was always bright purple. One day when Chris Draffen sat down in the freshly serviced potty someone slipped up behind and dropped a rock down the vent pipe. From the way Chris hollered when that rock hit the water, I think it must have done a pretty good job of painting his ass purple. Chris always thought that I dropped the rock, but I'm just going to stick with "someone".

*   *   *   *   *

A couple of weeks after that I sat down in the potty one morning and almost immediately I heard a truck start. That wasn't unusual at that time of day, so I didn't think much about it. Pretty soon I heard gravel crunching, and I thought they were driving awfully close to the john. About that time there was a thump, and the potty rocked a little bit. Chris had put the front bumper of the tender truck against the door of the potty, and then he went in the trailer and sat down and drank coffee with Steve.

A porta-potty isn't where I would choose to spend a lot of time, but there wasn't anything I could do about it, so I just tried to get comfortable until Chris decided to come back. Porta-potty's are definitely not air-conditioned, and I'll guaran-damn-tee I was ready to get out of that hot son-of-a-bitch by the time Chris moved the truck!

*   *   *   *   *

When I worked for MFA we had a few feed customers that no-one wanted to fool with. One afternoon when Jason Wolf returned from a particularly difficult delivery, he walked into the mill and said, "I hate to haul feed to that stupid bastard." Everyone chimed in "Yeah, that stupid bastard, he's really a stupid bastard, nobody wants to haul feed to that stupid bastard!"

That remark back-fired on Jason. He was nick-named "Stupid Bastard" for as long as he worked at MFA, and he still is "Stupid Bastard" whenever one of us runs into him somewhere. When Jason quit MFA he went to work driving a bulk-milk truck. Mike Anderson was driving down I-70 one day in the feed truck when he started hearing clanging noises. He thought the engine was blowing up. He glanced to his left and Stupid Bastard was passing him and flinging empty soda cans out of the window and bouncing them off the feed truck. Mikey said, "That Stupid Bastard."

When Stephen was 9 or 10 years old I took him and his Farmall C to Pilot Grove for a tractor pull. There were lots of people around, so I told Stephen I would drive his tractor from my trailer to the scales. He was standing on the draw bar, holding onto the back of the seat. Before we got to the scales we came across Jason and his girlfriend standing in the path, so when I got pretty close to them I yelled, "Get out of the way, you Stupid Bastard." Jason said, "I'll get out of the way when I'm ready, you stupid bastard." Stephen's eyes were big and he asked me "Paw-Paw, do you know him?" I said, "Yeah, young'un, I do and he's a real stupid bastard." As soon as I got off the tractor, Jason started grinning. We shook hands, then stood there and talked for 15 or 20 minutes. The longer we talked the better Stephen felt about things. He'd been afraid that his Paw-Paw was going to get in a fight, and he wasn't quite ready for that.

*   *   *   *   *

Early one morning Harry Mutter headed east on Highway 40 with a load of fertilizer on the black Kenworth. Just before he got to the top of the viaduct hill a deer ran in front of him and he smacked the hell out of it. The left front fender and the grill were wiped out, and the bumper was driven back into the tire. Steve Crowley hooked onto the bumper with the ton truck and pulled it off the tire far enough that Harry could limp the truck back to the fertilizer plant. He off-loaded onto another truck and made his delivery with no further problems.

By the time Harry got to work the next morning, someone had cut a picture of a road-killed deer out of the Missouri Conservationist and glued it onto the fender of the Kenworth. They also used a label maker and just above the door handle on the driver's side it said, "DEER SLAYER".

About a week later, I was on my way to work when a deer ran across the road in front of me in almost exactly the same spot. I missed it, but the car coming the other way hit it and rolled it end over end down a steep bank onto the Katy Trail. The car pulled off onto the shoulder, and I backed up and asked the young lady driving if she was all right. She said she was fine, but she wanted to know if she had killed the deer. I said, "Yes ma'am, you got him good. He won't run in front of anyone else."

She started bawling, and with tears streaming down her face she said, "The poor little deer didn't do anything wrong, I didn't aim to hurt him." I said, "Ma'am, you're okay, your car can be fixed, and that stupid deer isn't going to cause someone to have a wreck. You did good, I'm proud of you".

She started bawling again, and said, "That poor, poor, little deer." I said, "Ma'am, are you really sure that you're okay?" She said, "I'm fine, but I killed that poor little deer." I'd heard about all of that silly crap that I wanted to hear, so I said, "Yes ma'am, you sure did, you killed that sorry, no good, son-of-a-bitch dead!" And as I pulled onto the road and headed for Boonville she was bawling again. I don't know what in the hell that woman would have done if something bad had actually happened.

DAMN DEER! Little truck November 29th, 2003, big truck December 6th, 2003, five miles further down the same road.

*   *   *   *   *

One morning Gene Otis tossed a shovel on the side of my nurse truck and said if I ran across some little river birches while I was spraying in the bottom, that Becky (his wife) would like to have 3 or 4 to set out in their yard.

A few days later, I ran across some nice little birches about waist tall, and dug 5 or 6 of them. I tossed them on the wooden rack on the side of the truck and hauled them back to town. I didn't think about the fact that over the years there had probably been $5,000 worth of chemical spilled on that rack. I should have wrapped those roots with something to protect them, because they soaked up enough chemical that the trees all died the first year.

*   *   *   *   *

Lonnie Winn had the weakest stomach of any grown man that I ever knew. Steve Crowley and I ruined his lunch more than once, just because we could. Occasionally when we would get lunch at Snoddy's Store, I would get a quart of buttermilk to drink with my lunch. Lonnie couldn't understand how I could stand to drink "That nasty-assed buttermilk."

One day Steve, Lonnie and I had picked up lunch at Snoddy's, and when we got back to the fertilizer plant Lonnie walked into the trailer and as usual, sat down at Steve's desk before Steve got there. After Steve and I sat down in the loafers' chairs I opened my buttermilk and held it up to my face. I closed one eye and peered into the carton with the other one. Lonnie asked me what I was doing and I replied, "I'm checking to see if this crap is green, that's the only way I can tell if it's spoiled."

Lonnie gagged and headed for the door. Steve and I had finished our lunch before Lonnie ever came back into the trailer.

*   *   *   *   *

Chris Draffen's ruts, July 2000.
I knew there was a bad seep in this field, but I forgot to tell Chris it was there.

Chris Draffen and Steve Crowley, July 2000

One summer Chris Draffen and I were spraying beans on the old Vandiver Place, north east of S&S Seed Farm. The neighbors always referred to the place as "the rattlesnake farm." About the middle of the afternoon, Scott Clifford brought us a truckload of water so we could keep spraying. I knew Scottie was scared of snakes, so I warned him that if he went wandering around while he was waiting for us he should be sure to keep an eye out for rattlesnakes.

The next time we came to the truck to refill Scottie had climbed up on top, and was setting cross-legged on top of that 3,000-gallon tank; he looked like a big Buddha Statue setting up there. After we finished spraying and were getting ready to head back to Boonville, Scottie climbed in the truck and sat down, and then I casually mentioned that the only person that I actually knew of who had gotten snake-bit on that farm had climbed into his truck to take a load of wheat to town, and a snake that was coiled up under the seat bit him on the leg.

Scottie fell out of that cab and went back to the top of the tank. Chris and I had to completely remove everything from under the seat and then beat on the seat with a stick before Scottie would ever climb back into that truck. He didn't really see the humor in it, but Chris and I thought it was pretty funny.

*   *   *   *   *

Ronnie Anderson couldn't stand Scott Clifford, and Scottie couldn't stand Ronnie. They were cross-ways at all times about something. That wasn't any big deal until Mike Ashley left as manager, and MFA promoted Ronnie from applicator to manager. After that their arguments got a little bit more one-sided.

It didn't matter what Scott did, Ronnie didn't like it, and he rode Scottie pretty hard most of the time. One morning Scottie and Ronnie had another one of their yelling contests. When Scottie walked out of the office he looked like he was about to explode. I was just outside when he walked out and he said, "Alan, I think I'm just about to get fired, I'm going to give the assholes two weeks' notice. Come on in with me, I want someone to witness the fact that I gave notice before Ronnie fired me."

That caused another good yelling match, and I just stood back and listened. By the time the yelling was over, Scottie had turned in his 2 weeks' notice and was suddenly going to get sick and draw three days of sick-leave, and then take the seven days' vacation that he had coming. He picked up everything that he had laying around and headed toward his truck to go home and draw MFA money for the next two weeks. That suited Ronnie, 'cause he wanted Scottie gone just as bad as Scottie wanted to be gone.

While Scottie was on vacation, he talked to the manager at Tipton MFA, and the Monday after his vacation ended he went to work at Tipton. Scottie got a raise, it was a lot closer to his home, and he didn't get hollered at for no reason anymore. "Special Ed" never did like "his people" quitting during busy season, and he wasn't real happy about Scott going to work at another MFA location, but there wasn't much he could do about it except bitch and gripe, which he did. That's been over ten years ago, and the last I heard Scottie was still at Tipton. I think he came out way ahead on that deal.

*   *   *   *   *

Me spreading lime at Howard Draffen's farm, November 1999

Old Paul worked at the fertilizer plant part time for several years. He was probably the most gullible person I ever met. It didn't matter what you told him, if you could keep a straight face, he would believe you, at least momentarily.

One day I was talking about the old farm on Bearfield Road where I was raised and I mentioned the fact that every field on the farm had at least one rocky spot, and some fields had two or three. Paul was used to river bottom ground with no rocks, so he asked me how the rocks got there. I explained that Boone County was mostly glacial soil, and I told him that the glaciers dumped the rocks as it moved through.

Paul looked at me and asked, "There was a glacier on your farm?" I replied, "Why hell yes, when I was a kid there were still big chunks of ice on the north slopes that hadn't thawed yet." Paul said, "There was?...For sure?...Oh come on now!"

There's Something There

The material in this chapter is a little bit different than what I usually write about. Some of you might read this and say, "I believe the old man's losing it," and others might say "Hell, he never had it to begin with." And they might be right, but I'll guaran-damn-tee there's something there.

Angels, spirits, spooks, ghosts, goblins or visions, it doesn't matter what you choose to call them, they are there and they're definitely real. I don't know what people who have had formal religious training think about it, but I don't think I could ever be trained enough to make me believe that there's not something there.

*   *   *   *   *

Strange things have been happening in the old house on Bearfield Road for many years. My cousin, Esther, said that Mom told her that not long after Grandpap died, she and Pappy were sitting in the living room one evening after supper when they heard footsteps. Pappy started to get up, but then they realized it was Grandpap walking around in the front bedroom. Mom told Esther that the speed and rhythm were exactly the same they had grown used to hearing over the years when Grandpap moved around in the front of the house at bedtime. That was the only time they ever heard the footsteps. Pappy said, "Well Margaret, apparently Pap forgot something he needed, and he had to come back for it." There's something there.

*   *   *   *   *

When Greg started high school at Rock Bridge he was on the Junior Varsity football team. They had a game one afternoon when I was combining soybeans so I didn't attend, Marcia and Jeff went by themselves.

I was cutting in the big bottom at Schwabe's (that NASCAR driver Carl Edwards owns now) and I was about halfway across the field when I suddenly said "Son-of-a-bitch, Greg just broke his damn arm!" I assumed that he did it playing football, but the details just weren't there. I couldn't do anything about it, so I went ahead cutting beans 'til around 9:00pm. When I got home and walked in the house, Marcia and Jeff were sitting at the kitchen table. After they said "Hi" I asked where Greg was. Jeff said, "He's laying on his bed, guess what he did?" I replied. "He broke his arm." They both stared at me, and Marcia finally asked me how I found out. When I told her and then told her what time it happened, they just sat there and stared at me some more. I was right about the time, but I was actually about 2" off on the break, he broke his wrist instead of his arm. Anyhow, there's definitely something there.

*   *   *   *   *

Bill Schuler and I farmed the old Schwabe Place together for 20 years. Bill was big, rough and tough, and at one time before he started putting on weight, he could probably have whipped most anyone in Boone County.

In the late 1970's a body, (actually a skeleton) was discovered in Little Cedar Creek where it runs through the Schwabe Farm. Bill never stayed and worked on that farm after dark again. He said, "I'm not giving those god damn spooks a chance to get me." I don't 'spect they were looking for Bill, but he was convinced there was something there, and he wasn't about to make it easy for them.

*　　*　　*　　*　　*

After Pappy died in 1982, mom spent the next three months looking for his birth certificate. It wasn't with any of their other important papers, and she had about given up on ever finding it.

Mom said one night around 1:00am she felt the bed shake and when she woke up she saw Pappy standing at the foot of the bed, gently shaking it. He smiled and said, "Margaret, it's in the box in the gun cabinet." She said, "Thank you, Will," and he smiled at her again and just disappeared. She immediately got up and went to the gun cabinet and there in the box was Pappy's birth certificate. There's something there.

*　　*　　*　　*　　*

The old house on Bearfield Road where Sis and I were raised was built in the early 1870's. My Great-Grandparents lived there, Grandpap and his first wife lived there for a short time until she died, Grandpap and Grandma lived there for 60 some years, Pappy, Uncle Edward and Aunt Mary were raised there, and Pappy and Momma lived there for 40 years. After Pappy died, Momma lived there for another 25 years. Over the past 140 years there's no telling how many family members and friends spent time in the house.

Sis and I never noticed anything because we were born into the house and we were supposed to be there. However, the former residents are always curious when someone new moves in. There's something there.

*   *   *   *   *

After Mom died, Jeff moved into the old house. Before long his girlfriend Kelli and her son, Junior, were staying with him. They put Junior's bed in the "north hall," which had been Grandpap and Grandma's bedroom when I was a kid. Nearly every night for a while, a few minutes after he went to bed Junior would come back into the living room and curl up on the couch. One night Kelli told him to go back to bed and go to sleep. He said, "I can't go to sleep, they won't shut up." She asked him who wouldn't shut up and he said, "Those people, they just keep whispering."

Jeff said one afternoon he laid down in that room to take a nap and just before he dozed off he heard whispering in the background. He couldn't tell what they were saying, he said it was like they were just out of sight and having a real quiet conversation. They weren't used to the new residents yet, and they were checking them out. There's something there.

This isn't the only house that has spirits, and many other houses that did have spirits have been torn down over the years. I can't help but wonder, where do they go when their old houses are finally torn down?

*   *   *   *   *

After Sis and I sold 20 acres with the house and buildings to Boys and Girls Town in 2014, they told me I could salvage anything I wanted because they were going to demolish the buildings and haul them to the city dump.

One afternoon Jeff and I took the shutters off the front of the old house, and then went inside and started removing the porcelain doorknobs. When we walked into the North Hall we stopped and looked around, then I told Jeff that I had come by a few days earlier and told the old people that we weren't trying to disrespect their home, but that it was so old that it was just used up. I told them they had done a good job of caring for it over the years, but they didn't have to watch out for it any longer if they didn't want to.

As we headed into the next room, Jeff said "Yeah, I came by and talked to them too, I thought they deserved to know what's going on."

There's something there!

*   *   *   *   *

A few years ago Marcia and I talked about being buried in the Fortney Cemetery. As usual she was thinking about everyone else and she said, "Oh Alan, it would just be too much trouble for everyone." I replied that it wouldn't really be that much trouble, and since we didn't figure that we'd have to make that decision for a long time we just left it at that.

When Marcia died un-expectedly on December 29th, 2012, I told Greg, Jeff, and all of the Grandkids that if no one had any objections I wanted to bury my baby in the Fortney Cemetery. No one did, so I made the decision to have the burial there, and it wouldn't have been too much trouble IF the damn weather had co-operated. However, the day before the funeral it was snowing and sleeting so hard that the grave crew couldn't even get to Columbia, so Parker Funeral Service owner Bruce Rice and I decided to hold the funeral service, but postpone the burial.

Clint, Taylor, and Leah were all here on funeral leave from the Service, and had to leave Columbia Friday afternoon, so Bruce told me that he would somehow make it work for Friday morning. He got the crew lined up to open the grave at 2:00 Thursday afternoon, but they were late, and by the time they finally arrived at 4:45 it was getting dark. I was a nervous wreck, the snow and horse manure was thawing, and brown water was running through the barn lot as they unloaded and we slogged through snow, slush, horse manure and mud to make our way up the hill to the cemetery. By the time they got lined up with the grave site, they had the headlights on and one worker was holding a big spotlight.

Greg, Jamie, and I were standing in the snow and the slush, watching them dig the grave in the dark, when I suddenly started laughing. Jamie gave me a funny look and asked, "Paw-Paw, what are you laughing about?" I said, "Jamie, I just saw Marcia, as plain as I'm seeing you, and she was smiling one of those big Marcia smiles, and she said, "Alan, I told you it would be too much trouble." I replied, "Maybe for some people, Babe, but not when it's for you." There's something there.

*   *   *   *   *

Marcia and Cloe, Stephen's old Bassett hound, were pretty good buddies. If Cloe wasn't outside she usually spent most of her time laying next to Marcia's chair in the sewing room, computer room, or wherever. After Marcia died, Cloe wandered around the house for two or three weeks, whining and looking for her. Every time Cloe would wake up from a nap she would check all of the likely places, and then set down in front of the couch in the family room and beller.

Cloe always spends the night in the house, and if I get up by 6:30 she never bothers me, but if I sleep a little bit late she'll wake me up to let her out. She meanders along, and I'll usually pass her and have the door open when she gets there. About three months after Marcia died Cloe woke me one night, and when I looked at the clock it was 2:00am (that is the exact time that Marcia had the aneurism that caused her death). I said, "Old pup, do you need to go out?" She spun around and headed down the hall with her tail wagging from side to side as fast as she could wag it. By the time I got to the door she had her head jammed against it and was pushing so hard that I couldn't hardly get the door open. I flipped on the outside lights and opened the storm door.

Old Cloe usually takes so long going out the door that I'll give her a little push so I can shut the door and keep the cold out, but that night she busted out the door and stood looking east with her tail wagging so hard she couldn't hardly stand up. I figured Greg's big dog, Yogi, was making a night time visit and when I stepped out to tell him hi, I saw Marcia standing in front of the garage looking at me. I said, "Hi, Babe," and she gave me a big old smile, held her arms out and then just disappeared. Cloe looked at me like "What the hell just happened?," and then walked over and started circling around the driveway. She couldn't pick up a scent anywhere, so she went over to where I'd seen Marcia, sniffed that spot for a moment, let out a big sigh, then laid down on her stomach with her chin on her paws. I stood there for a little bit with tears in my eyes, then I went back in the house.

It was pretty chilly that night, so about 15 minutes later I checked to see if Cloe was ready to come back inside. She just looked at me, then laid her head back down and ignored me. When I got up at 6:30 she was still asleep, laying on her stomach on that cold concrete, with her head on her paws. She spent most of the day right there, sometimes sleeping, sometimes laying there with her head up, looking around in all directions, wondering where Marcia went.

Cloe and I both guaran-damn-tee there's something there, and I'm sure 'nuff glad there is. God, Baby, I miss you!

Odds and Ends

Did you ever notice that a rich crook dies just as dead as a poor honest man? He just doesn't get nearly as much respect after he's gone.

*　　*　　*　　*　　*

When someone says something about me getting old I reply "Yeah, but if Larry Atterberry can make it at his age I shouldn't have any problems." Damn, that man is old, old, OLD!

*　　*　　*　　*　　*

The old timers were real sticklers about their buildings being square and true, but that sure didn't carry over to their cemeteries. The stones in the Fortney Cemetery aren't really lined up, they run at least a foot or two out of line one way or the other. Also, some of the stones are at the head of the graves and some are at the foot. It's almost like they threw a shovel over the fence and dug where ever it landed. It sure makes it hard to decide who is buried where. Add in all the unmarked graves, and it's pretty much a hodge-podge.

*　　*　　*　　*　　*

How long has it been since you've heard anyone talk about feeding "fodder" to their cows? Does anyone even remember what "fodder" is?

*   *   *   *   *

Marcia died when I was 70 years old; assuming that I'll live as long as most of my relatives did, it's going to be a damn long 20 some years without my Baby.

*   *   *   *   *

When my grandson, Stephen, lived in Sturgeon he borrowed a couple of Pappy's old frog gigs from me one evening. Some punk-assed kid up at Sturgeon latched on to them and kept them for himself. I hope the sorry little prick slips and falls backwards on them some night, and runs them up his thieving ass!

*   *   *   *   *

When I was writing my first book Marcia thought it was about the neatest thing that had ever happened. However, each time she would proofread a few pages, she would ask me "Alan, do you have to cuss so much?" I'd say "Yeah, Babe, it seems to fit in pretty good most of the time." It did then and it still does; sorry about that.

Writing this book without Marcia's encouragement is a totally different experience. It's not nearly as much fun, but it gives me something to do, so I guess as long as I keep remembering this stuff I'll keep writing it down. I miss you, Baby, this one's for you.

*   *   *   *   *

Whenever Marcia boiled a country ham, she always added two large cans of pineapple juice to the water while the ham was starting, and then added another can later after the water had boiled down some. One year at Thanksgiving, I was getting a ham ready for her to cook, and I was ready to add the pineapple juice. Some of the grandkids were at the house that morning, and I asked one of them to get me a "church key" out of the kitchen cabinet. They had no idea what I wanted.

Years ago, anytime someone stopped at the beer store for a six pack, the clerk would automatically ask if you needed a "church key." A church key is just a simple combination can/bottle opener. One end popped the cap off sodas or bottled beer, and the other end made a neat, triangle shaped hole in the old flat-topped steel beer cans. Occasionally you would get a plain one, but most of them advertised Budweiser, Falstaff, or some other brand of beer. You can still get the openers at Walmart and other stores; I've got one in the cabinet now that is stamped Hueck, USA. It works just fine, but I kinda wish I'd kept a couple of the old advertising "church keys," just for the hell of it.

*   *   *   *   *

I was sitting in a Cafe in Memphis, Missouri one evening, eating supper with Gene Brown when a local farmer walked up to our table. He talked to Gene for a minute, then he looked at me and said, "If you lie a little bit everyday you'll eventually get good at it, just like him." Seems like everyone knows Gene.

*   *   *   *   *

If you see Dane Chandler ask him if he still remembers the words to that sweet little nursery rhyme, "PISS POT

PETE." He damn sure knew them when he was 5 years old.

*   *   *   *   *

When Momma was in the Nursing Home she was slipping so fast that occasionally I could see the difference from day to day. Sometime in the spring I got a letter from my cousin, Bud Middleton, and he said that he and Rose were coming to Columbia in the fall, and he was looking forward to visiting Mom. When I wrote him back I said that Mom was going downhill a little bit every day, and I hoped she was still here when they came in the fall, but that I really wouldn't count on it.

Bud called me a few days later to get directions to the Nursing Home. He said he was driving to Columbia just to see Mom, and he was going to spend three days with her. Bud made the drive from Florida, and that visit made Mom's summer. About six weeks later she passed away.

*   *   *   *   *

When our Granddaughter, Leah, joined the Marines, someone asked her why she chose the Marines. She said, "Taylor is in the Army, Clint is in the Navy, and I'm tougher than they are, so I joined the Marines." I don't know if she's tougher than they are, but she's damn sure tough enough that she made it in the Marines. I'm proud of you, Little Girl!

*   *   *   *   *

I suppose telemarketers have been around almost as long as the telephone. As far as I'm concerned they're all just a big pain in the ass.

Several years after Pappy passed away, Mom answered the phone one morning, and a very cheerful voice asked her "May I speak to William, please?" Mom said he wasn't available, and asked if she could take a message. The guy told her he had talked to Pappy the week before about buying some kind of rip-off crap, and Pappy was really interested in the item and wanted to place an order, and he asked Mom if she wanted to go ahead and order while they were on the phone.

Mom asked him "You talked to Will about this last week?" When the guy assured her that he had, Mom said "Oh, I wish you would tell me how you did that, Will has been dead for almost four years, and I sure would love to talk to him." SLAM! That was the last she heard out of that lying son-of-a-bitch.

*　　*　　*　　*　　*

Is anyone out there wearing a shirt that's had the collar turned? Does anyone even remember what it means to "Turn the Collar?"

*　　*　　*　　*　　*

Several years before Momma passed away she got all of the family together and put names on furniture, guns, dishes and all of the other assorted treasures that were in the house. When Mom finally had to go to a nursing home we moved stuff out of the house as quick as we could, before people realized that the house was vacant, and decided to help themselves.

One afternoon my nephew Karl DeMarce, and his Father-in-law Frank Russell, came by the house to load Karl's stuff and take it to Memphis, Missouri. Karl has a pretty impressive "Duck Dynasty" type beard, and he was wearing bib overalls that day. Jeff was helping us and his girlfriend, Kelli, came by before we finished. Somehow no introductions got made, and after Karl and Frank left Kelli asked "Jeff, who was the Amish guy that helped you load the furniture?" Jeff said, "He's not Amish, that's my Dad's nephew, he's a judge."

I don't believe I ever saw an Amish Circuit Judge, but if you don't know him, Karl does look kind of Amish.

*   *   *   *   *

When my some sort of a distant cousin Roger Wilson agreed to write the foreword for this book, I thought "Well, this will be the first book ever published with the foreword written by an honest politician."

*   *   *   *   *

Marcia was 16 years old when I met her in 1959, and she was already collecting pretty "stuff." It took her 50 some years to accumulate everything in this sale, and it took the auctioneer just over 6 hours to sell it. I hope the new owners get as much enjoyment out of it over the years as Marcia did. I miss you, Babe!

Estate Auction popsicle

Saturday January 4, 10:00
VFW Post 280 Hall
1509 Ashley Street
Columbia, Missouri
Seller: Marcia Easley Estate

AUCTIONEER'S NOTE: This is an outstanding auction that you will not want to miss! Crocks, advertising, oak items, and signs are all superb and in excellent condition. There are some rare examples and some truly unusual items. Come join us for a fun New Year's auction!

Pictures and complete catalog with sale order available at blackandgoldauctions.com

A Few Highlights:

Red Wing 5, 10, and 30 Gallon Jars
Red Wing 20 Pound Butter Crock
Salt Glazed Stoneware
Advertising Crocks
Sue Gerard Pottery (30+)
Strong-Heart and 50+ Coffee Tins
Coca-Cola Glo-Dial Neon Clock
25+ Tin, Wood, Cardboard and Porcelain Advertising Signs:
Coke, RC Cola, Pepsi, Squirt, Kist, Columbia Bicycles, Motorola, US Army, Globe Paint, Yellow Cab
Salesman's Samples
J & P Coats Spool Cabinets
Oak File Cabinets and Boxes
Barrister Bookcases
Toy Cookstoves and Furniture
Sericels
Tin Trucks
Much, Much, More!

BLACK & GOLD AUCTIONS
CHUCK PRICE
blackandgoldauctions.com 573-445-7333
7873

*   *   *   *   *

When I was a kid, Joe Crane had a shepherd-type dog named "Piddler." Joe said, "I do all the work, and the dad-blamed dog just piddles around."

*   *   *   *   *

If you have three grandkids coming in from the service at the same time, Bryan McHugh is a pretty good person to know.

I made one phone call, and he fixed me up with twenty some pounds of frozen calf nuts. If we feed those kids like that the whole time they're here, we might have trouble getting them to leave.

*   *   *   *   *

Previously published in "The Missouri Conservationist," used with permission.

The sheer volume of mushrooms available in 1991 made conditions good for teaching the fine art of mushroom hunting to a whole generation of youth who have grown up without participating in this time-honored tradition.

There are many ways of hunting mushrooms. Probably the most popular is "stick hunting," walking slowly through the woods with a stick, while gently brushing back leaves and trash to expose the culinary delights hiding beneath. That way works fine for a young person, but after you get old and lazy you tend to look for an easier method.

"Still hunting" is one of my personal favorites. Everyone knows that mushrooms don't grow like common plants. They pop through the ground in their full-grown state. Anything the size of a mushroom is bound to make some noise when it pops up, thus still hunting is a viable alternative for anyone who doesn't want to do a lot of unnecessary walking. You merely go into the woods, locate a likely mushroom area, then sit down and get comfortable.

It is important to listen closely, because small mushrooms don't make a lot of noise coming through the ground. They sound about like a .22-caliber shot going off, and create a minimal amount of ground disturbance. However, the big ones are a different story. They sound like a 12-gauge shotgun, and throw dirt 5 to 10 feet into the air. This makes it imperative that you wear heavy clothing and head protection, such as a construction hard hat; serious injury can occur from falling clods. I once sat down in a rocky area just before a large patch of mushrooms popped up, and I suffered severe bruises to my ego and parts of my anatomy.

Several years ago I heard about a mushroom dog. By the time I verified the rumor and located the dog's owner, mushroom season was over and I was unable to see the dog in action. However, I took the owner at his word, since mushroom hunters, like fishermen, are not prone to lie. We agreed on a price and I headed home with my new dog, Lacks. His previous owner said, "He isn't really stupid, but he lacks just a little." Lacks had one serious flaw as a mushroom dog. He was half bird dog and half mutt and he was still-mouthed. He would point mushrooms, but wouldn't bark "treed" when he located a mushroom. This made hunting with him harder than stick hunting, since I had to move fast enough to keep him in sight or I would miss his points.

Lacks disappeared one day and couldn't be found anywhere. Finally a neighbor called and said Lacks had been on point in his front yard for three days. I went to get him, and he was pointing a concrete mushroom yard decoration. After this I decided to sell Lacks and train my own mushroom dog. Since I was already the owner of a smart and beautiful Black and Tan/Walker cross, with an excellent mouth, I decided to train her.

Old Leon (yes, Leon is a female, but that's another story) already barked at squirrels, cars and night noises so adding mushrooms wasn't too hard. She can scout out a patch of mushrooms in nothing flat, and then bark treed. She has just one drawback - a taste for mushrooms. She barks until I arrive at the patch, then she eats while I pick. This cuts my share in half, but it still beats stick hunting.

DAMN NICE MUSHROOMS! Marcia and Ol' Leon found these, spring 1994.

Another method is "sack hunting." This requires three or four people, but can produce large numbers of mushrooms. You go into the woods with your snipe sack and hold it open while your helpers circle around and drive the mushrooms toward you. When snipe hunting, the novice usually holds the sack, but I always hold the sack when mushroom hunting because I can stay in one place and let the kids do the walking. The only problem with sack hunting is that if a large number of mushrooms come toward you at the same time a few might slip by the sides of the sack. However, this isn't really harmful, since you need to leave a few breeding pairs anyway.

There are one or two other minor methods that can be used, but I don't have time to discuss them right now. I hear Leon barking, and I think I'll go mushroom hunting.

Note: You'll just have to use your own judgement as to whether or not you think everything in this story "sure 'nuff happened." It's been a long time, and I just can't remember for sure.

* * * * *

I recently bought a rear blade at Terry Rowland's farm auction up towards Harrisburg. I didn't have my trailer with me, so Brent Voorhies offered to take the blade down the road to his house so it wouldn't disappear before I came after it. That was pretty nice of him, but I don't know why the hell he didn't just bring it on down to my place while he had it loaded, it wouldn't have been but 20 some miles out of his way. You didn't think of that, did you Brent?

* * * * *

Things in Boone County turn in a pretty tight circle. When I was in grade school, Gene Melloway and I attended Grindstone together for a couple of years. In 2014, his son and grandsons did a bunch of work on my Dodge dually, in their Body Shop east of Hallsville. They did a right decent job, too.

* * * * *

There's always something going on to keep life interesting. Recently Jeff was watching TV on a Saturday night, when he suddenly heard an engine revving up, then there was a loud thump and some grinding noises.

By the time he got his boots on and made it out to the road, the driver was walking around shining his flashlight into the road ditch. Jeff asked him, "Did my mailbox jump out in front of you, Officer?"

A Boone County Deputy Sheriff had run into the ditch, jumped Jeff's driveway, wiped out the mailbox, and pretty much destroyed a good patrol car in the process. He told Jeff that an oncoming car had forced him off the road. BULL'S ASS! I don't know how many times he heard that excuse, but I'll bet that he never believed it any more than we did.

The Sheriff's Dept. is insured by MoPerm Ins. out of Jefferson City. If you ever have to deal with that bunch of jerks, I hope you come out a lot better than we did. Thanks a damn bunch, MoPerm!

$$* \quad * \quad * \quad * \quad *$$

Zane Dodge proof-read some of this stuff for me. After he finished reading he said "Plow-Boy, I believe you've got some words in there that Mr. Webster doesn't have in his book." I replied, "Hell, Zane, I don't know over 5 or 6 people who can read without moving their lips, so it doesn't really matter what words I use, they're going to figure out what I mean eventually."

Time Flies

In my first book I mentioned that Babe Manns was one of the few people who had lived in the Olivet Neighborhood longer than James Earl Grant and me. Babe died the same month the book was published. He was one hell of a good neighbor and he'll be missed. Time Flies.

*   *   *   *   *

Fred and Kathi Vom Saal, Joe and Corienne Remieke, Tom and Cindi Stewart, Tom and Carol Norling, and Bea Judd Bradshaw are about the only ones left in the Bearfield Road area that are really neighbors. There are others that I wave at, and some that I cuss at when they fly down that narrow-assed blacktop 50 miles per hour, but the days of knowing all of your neighbors in that area are about done. Time Flies!

*   *   *   *   *

Mom told me once that when Grandpap was well up in his 90's, he said that it gets really lonesome when you get old. He told her that you still know a lot of people, but there's no one left that you used to know.

When mom was in the nursing home for a year before she died, she told me that she realized what he was talking about. She said getting old beat the alternative up to a certain point, but that you could carry it on for too long.

I don't really feel like I'm very old, but Marcia is gone, Pappy and Mom, Nanny and Paw, (Marcia's Parents) all of my aunts and uncles, a bunch of my cousins, my brother-in-law Jim DeMarce, lots of good neighbors, quite a few of my high school classmates and a hell of a bunch of good dogs are gone too. Damn it anyhow, what the hell happened? Both of our sons are older than I ought to be, the grandkids are all grown, and I've got two great grandsons and a great granddaughter. Time flies, and that ain't no shit.

Me, Marcia, Leah, Taylor, and Greg

Greg, Leah, Marcia, Taylor, and Clint

Marcia and Leah

Taylor, Justin, and me, Christmas 2001

Leah and Daz at the 2008 Boone County Fair 4H Horse Show.

*   *   *   *   *

I think I'm just about done now. I've pretty much told you everything I know, but before I quit I'm going to leave you with a list of things I've learned over the years:

1) Good friends are forever!
2) Never, ever, under any circumstances, give your wife a new garbage disposer as an Anniversary present.
3) Never, ever, under any circumstances, install it a year and a half later as a birthday present. Just trust me on these two, I know!
4) If the temperature gauge on a tractor or truck says "HOT" at all times, that tractor or truck will eventually be "HOT." (Damned expensive lesson).
5) If you forget to put the axe on the tractor when you go to cut ice for the cows, don't look at the pond and say, "I don't think that's very deep, I'll just drive the front wheels out on the ice and break it." You'll sure 'nuff break it, but I'll guaran-damn-tee it will be deeper than you thought it was. The tractor will go in over the hubs, and it will freeze in solid before you get back the next morning with another tractor.
6) If your locally owned bank changes ownership, it won't be an improvement.
7) A good honest politician can't accomplish very much, but one of those sorry crooked bastards can screw up a whole bunch.
8) If it's 10° below zero when you walk in the house after feeding, don't say "That's the last time I'm stepping foot out of this house today." It don't work that way! The yearlings will break through the ice and fall in the pond, some idiot will drive through your fence right next to a busy highway, or your neighbor will get stuck and need a pull. Whatever the reason, you WILL get out of the house again.

9) A rich crook dies just as dead as a poor honest man, he just doesn't get nearly as much respect after he's gone.

And last but not least:

10)   Never try to cut a truckload of firewood if you have the shits!

Well I think that's just about all that I know. If I pull anything else out of my head it might cave in, so I'm going to quit before it does. I hope you've enjoyed my memories, because I've sure 'nuff enjoyed remembering the biggest part of them.

CPSIA information can be obtained
at www.ICGtesting.com
Printed in the USA
LVOW13*0343010717

540030LV00003B/3/P